T0340024

# Neoliberalism, Management and Religion

The use of non-secular, religious concepts in contemporary managerial discourse to legitimise leadership, organisation and work has been undertheorised. Concepts such as organisational soul, Spiritual Leadership, a wider deification (and demonisation) of leaders, and the mantra of individual freedom each evoke long religio-historical roots. The deployment of such terms in the present to (re)enrol people into the service of capitalism speaks both to high levels of religious belief worldwide and, more specifically, to a history of religion intersecting with public life in the US—a context pivotal in the development and dissemination of managerialism and wider neoliberal discourse.

Organised around the concepts of Gods, Devils, Soul and the Individual this book will show how these concepts are being employed in current managerial, leadership and organisation discourses, critically examine the religio-historical and philosophical roots of such, and demonstrate how the religio-historical and religio-philosophical can be brought into the lexicon of critical organisational scholarship to provide a language to engage with the non-secular legitimation of capitalism and its institutions.

In so doing, this book is a timely addition to organisation and management theory. It comes at a time that is witnessing a wider 'theological turn' in continental philosophy, mounting calls within organisation studies to 'take religion seriously', and an ongoing legitimation crisis of neoliberalism, one that is raising pivotal questions concerning how neoliberalism endures despite the deprivations and harms it occasions. This book is intended to be engaging and erudite, drawing upon a trans-disciplinary combination of popular and academic management texts, contemporary and classical philosophy, literature and religio-historical sources foundational in the construction of the Western subject.

**Edward Wray-Bliss** is an Associate Professor in the Department of Management, at the Faculty of Business and Economics, Macquarie University, Australia. His research examines the ethics and politics of organisational, managerial and academic life.

# Routledge Studies in Business Ethics

Originating from both normative and descriptive philosophical backgrounds, business ethics implicitly regulates areas of behaviour which influence decision making, judgment, behaviour and objectives of the leadership and employees of an organization. This series seeks to analyse current and leading edge issues in business ethics, and the titles within it examine and reflect on the philosophy of business, corporations and organizations pertaining to all aspects of business conduct. They are relevant to the conduct of both individuals and organizations as a whole.

Based in academic theory but relevant to current organizational policy, the series welcomes contributions addressing topics including: ethical strategy; sustainable policies and practices; finance and accountability; CSR; employee relations and workers' rights; law and regulation; economic and taxation systems.

**Restructuring Capitalism**
Materialism and Spiritualism in Business
*Rogene A. Buchholz*

**The Ethics of Neoliberalism**
The Business of Making Capitalism Moral
*Peter Bloom*

**Integrity in Business and Management**
*Edited by Marc Orlitzky and Manjit Monga*

**Corporate Social Responsibility in Emerging Economies**
Reality and Illusion
*Cosmina Leila Voinea and Cosmin Fratostiteanu*

**Neoliberalism, Management and Religion**
Re-examining the Spirits of Capitalism
*Edward Wray-Bliss*

For more information about this series please visit: www.routledge.com

# Neoliberalism, Management and Religion

## Re-examining the Spirits of Capitalism

Edward Wray-Bliss

NEW YORK AND LONDON

First published 2019
by Routledge
605 Third Avenue, New York, NY 10017

and by Routledge
2 Park Square, Milton Park, Abingdon, Oxon, OX14 4RN

First issued in paperback 2021

*Routledge is an imprint of the Taylor & Francis Group, an informa business*

© 2019 Taylor & Francis

The right of Edward Wray-Bliss to be identified as author of this work
has been asserted by him in accordance with sections 77 and 78 of the
Copyright, Designs and Patents Act 1988.

All rights reserved. No part of this book may be reprinted or reproduced
or utilised in any form or by any electronic, mechanical, or other means,
now known or hereafter invented, including photocopying and recording,
or in any information storage or retrieval system, without permission in
writing from the publishers.

*Trademark notice*: Product or corporate names may be trademarks or
registered trademarks, and are used only for identification and explanation
without intent to infringe.

*Library of Congress Cataloging-in-Publication Data*
Names: Wray-Bliss, Edward, author.
Title: Neoliberalism, management and religion : re-examining the spirits of
    capitalism / Edward Wray-Bliss.
Description: New York : Routledge, 2019. | Series: Routledge studies in
    business ethics | Includes bibliographical references and index.
Identifiers: LCCN 2018043290 | ISBN 9781138048379 (hardback) |
    ISBN 9781315114606 (ebook)
Subjects: LCSH: Business ethics. | Social responsibility of business. |
    Capitalism—Religious aspects. | Management—Religious aspects. |
    Neoliberalism.
Classification: LCC HF5387 .W73 2019 | DDC 330.12/2—dc23
LC record available at https://lccn.loc.gov/2018043290

ISBN 13: 978-0-367-78682-3 (pbk)
ISBN 13: 978-1-138-04837-9 (hbk)

Typeset in Sabon
by Apex CoVantage, LLC

# Contents

# Acknowledgements

Earlier versions of some passages and arguments contained in this work appear in the following: 'Redeeming Organizational Soul' *Organization* (April 2018); 'Leadership and the Deified/Demonic: A Cultural Critique of CEO Canonization' *Business Ethics: A European Review* (2012, 21/4); 'Critical Moral Philosophy and Management' in *The Springer Encyclopedia of Philosophy and Management* (forthcoming); 'Leadership, Ethical Sovereignty and the Politics of Property' in *The Routledge Companion to Ethics, Politics and Organizations*, ed. A. Pullen and C. Rhodes (Routledge 2015); and 'Ethical Philosophy, Organization Studies and Good Suspicions' in *The Routledge Companion to Philosophy in Organization Studies*, ed. R. Mir, H. Willmott and M. Greenwood (Routledge 2016).

I am very grateful to the lovely people at Routledge for commissioning and publishing this work; to the anonymous reviewers of the initial book proposal; to Carl Rhodes, Series Editor; to participants at the 2016 *Australasian Business Ethics Network* and 2017 *Critical Management Studies Conferences*; to Grant Michelson, for helpful suggestions on the proposal; to Macquarie University students doing units in *Leadership* and *Strategic Management*, whom I have tested some of the ideas on; and to Victoria Carruthers for her unwavering support, insightful comments and enthusiasm for what I have been writing.

# 1  Introduction

In the title of this study is used the somewhat pretentious phrase, the spirit of capitalism. What is to be understood by it?

Max Weber (1930[2001]:13), *The Protestant Ethic and the Spirit of Capitalism* (© Max Weber. Reproduced with permission of the Licensor through PLSclear)

For a number of years I have been researching and writing on matters of ethics as they relate to our organisational, and organised, lives. More recently this has taken me in the direction of thinking about the formative effects of religious and early philosophical discourse on ethical sensibility and subjectivity. And this has led to the book you have here, an examination of how religious concepts and ideas—the 'spirits' of this book's title—haunt, are summoned by and materialise in organisational, managerial and leadership texts and practices in the neoliberal present.

When the concept of 'spirit' is raised in relation to capitalism the foundational text is, of course, Max Weber's (1930[2001]) *The Protestant Ethic and the Spirit of Capitalism*. Weber observed that to be 'dominated by the making of money, by acquisition as the ultimate purpose in life' was the 'leading principle' (1930[2001]:18) of European and, especially, American capitalism (p. 16). What was 'most characteristic of the social ethic of capitalist culture', its 'fundamental basis' (p. 19), was that this drive to make 'more and more money, combined with the strict avoidance of all spontaneous enjoyment of life' had become a fundamental ethical duty, a calling even: such that the businessman lived 'for the sake of his business, rather than the reverse' (p. 32). And the spirit of capitalism did not just suffuse the businessman and owner of capital. Labour too came to 'be performed as if it were an absolute end itself, a calling' (p. 25).

For this spirit of capitalism to have arisen and taken hold, however, would not have been an easy or obvious outcome. Traditional religious and societal values stretching back as far as the ancient world would have looked upon the spirit that defines capitalism 'as the lowest sort of avarice and as an attitude entirely lacking in self-respect' (p. 21). Furthermore, even from the 'point of view of the happiness of, or utility to, the single individual' this spirit of ceaseless acquisition and endless disciplined labour in the service of such 'appears entirely transcendental and absolutely irrational' (p. 18). 'The spirit of capitalism', therefore, 'had to fight its way to supremacy against a whole world of hostile forces' (pp. 20–21), raising the question of how this idea, ethos, or *spirit*, could have arisen and taken such hold of European and, especially, American society.

Noting that the 'magical and religious forces, and the ethical ideas of duty based upon them, have in the past always been among the most important formative influences on conduct' (p. xxxix), Weber answered the above by tracing 'correlations' (p. 49) between the spirit of capitalism and historical forms of Protestant Christian religious belief. For instance, the Protestant Reformation's critique of monastic retreat from the world as exemplifying a Christian life served to construct dutiful ethical life as instead service to a worldly calling. John Calvin's teaching of the strict predestination of who would receive God's grace, and thereby eternal life, combined with the 'complete elimination of salvation through the Church and the sacraments' led to an 'unprecedented inner loneliness' for individuals (pp. 60 and 61). This all-but-unbearable existential loneliness led to a desperate search for some indication in the here-and-now of God's possible favour. Being 'blessed' with good fortune and wealth came to be this indication—later to be translated under capitalism to a veritable canonisation of the wealthy. And, though it was not specifically part of Calvin's own writing, the asceticism of the wider Calvinist movement encouraged the 'destruction of spontaneous, impulsive enjoyment' (p. 73). This cultivated the self-denying trait that served to inhibit the squandering of wealth and enabled accumulation and reinvestment amongst the early capitalists.

For Weber, then, Protestant Christianity cultivated ideals and practices of the self that—quite inadvertently—abetted the development of capitalism in Europe and its transplantation to, then exemplification by, America. Once it had reached maturity, capitalism became 'emancipated from its old supports' (p. 34), however, and no longer needed a religiously cultivated ethics of self-discipline and restraint. Indeed, Weber observes that those

> people filled with the spirit of capitalism today tend to be indifferent, if not hostile, to the Church. The thought of the pious boredom of paradise has little attraction for their active natures; religion appears to them as a means of drawing people away from labour in this world.
>
> (p. 32)

Capitalism now confronted humankind as an 'irresistible force . . . an iron cage' (p. 123) which imposed the necessary behaviour traits by virtue of the seduction of commodity consumption, the pursuit of wealth taking almost the character of sport (p. 124), or, for most of the population, through the

> technical and economic conditions of machine production which day-to-day determine the lives of all the individuals who are born into this mechanism, not only those directly concerned with economic acquisition, with irresistible force.
>
> (p. 123)

Shorn of the need for its formative religious foundations, the capitalist economy had become

> an immense cosmos into which the individual is born, and which presents itself to him, at least as an individual, as an unalterable order of things in which he must live. It forces the individual, in so far as he is involved in the system of market relationships, to conform to capitalist rules of action.
>
> (p. 19)

Weber's work is a major, canonical, text. And his use of the term *geist/ spirit*, though it has a longer history in philosophical work (e.g. Hegel 1806, 1807, see Chapter 4 *Soul*), has proved particularly evocative and haunting. We can see how Weber's spirit continues to summon new works by considering a few of the book-length studies of the spirit of capitalism currently in publication.

Liah Greenfeld's (2001) *The Spirit of Capitalism: Nationalism and Economic Growth*, for example, endorses Weber's conceptual approach—his seeking to understand 'the manner in which ideas become effective forces in history' (Weber 1930[2001]:48)—but argues that religion was the wrong set of originary ideas. Greenfeld argues that it was nationalism, rather than Protestantism, which was the driving force behind the development of capitalism. Undertaking an historical examination of nationalism in Britain, France, Germany, Japan and America, Greenfeld argues that it was English nationalism in particular, combining a focus upon economic achievement as a core element of a sense of national superiority with a form of liberal individualism as its mobilising force, that 'provided the original inspiration for the economics of sustained growth' (p. 25). For Greenfeld, the potency of such individualistic-civic nationalism, alongside its core contribution to Britain's early industrial 'economic miracle', made this a highly 'contagious' set of ideas and practices which later infected America so virulently.

In contrast to Greenfeld, Colin Campbell's (2005) *The Romantic Ethic and the Spirit of Modern Consumerism* endorses Weber's identification of Protestantism as a formative ethic of capitalism. For Campbell, however, Weber tells only half of the story. For not only were attitudes toward capital acquisition, production and labour transformed in capital-ism's infancy, so too was there a dramatic change in attitudes towards consumption—the necessary mirror side to what Campbell casts as Weber's spirit of capitalist *production*. For example, there was a veri-table consumer revolution in eighteenth-century England, and 'evidence strongly suggests that the consumer revolution was carried through by exactly those sections of English society with the strongest Puritan tradi-tions' (p. 31). This consumer revolution necessitated the rise of a mode of being—a spirit of consumerism—no less irrational or immoral for traditionalism as the spirit of capitalist production was in the centuries before. As per Weber, Campbell traces the spirit back to an historical, reli-gious, ethic. Rather than the Puritan ethic of self-restraint and asceticism, however, Campbell argues that a Romantic ethic—rooted in sentimental Pietistic Protestantism—unwittingly provided the foundations for the spirit of consumption. Love for Christ; the bitter-sweet pleasure of per-petual longing for salvation; the cult of sensibility for the beauty of God's creations; the worship of saints; and the driving of powerful emotions within, such that the individual must imaginatively construct their own passionate relationship with God, created the conditions for the Romantic ethic. And this ethic, argues Campbell, constructed a population able and desiring to imaginatively invest themselves in recurring longing for elusive emotional pleasure: the type of population necessary for the development of a spirit of endless modern consumerism.

Kathryn Blanchard's (2010) *The Protestant Ethic or the Spirit of Capitalism: Christians, Freedom, and Free Markets* examines, from an explicitly Christian perspective, the relationship of Protestant Christianity with capitalism. Alongside a rereading of Adam Smith, Chicago School economists and others, Blanchard revisits John Calvin's writings and counterpoises these with Weber's interpretations. For example, Blanchard argues that Weber cast Calvinists as ascetics who regarded as sinful the full enjoyment of the material world and that this laid down important conditions for the reinvestment rather than squander of gains necessary in the development of capitalism. Blanchard shows, though, that Calvin's works explicitly enjoined enjoyment of the created world, instructed the faithful not to contrive to create rules of piety around trivialities such as personal consumption, and 'boldly rejected ascetic ideals as the true measure of Christian perfection' (p. 22). Similarly, Blanchard argues that Weber identified in Calvinism the foundations of a calling to labour and to make money, whereas she argues that 'Calvin is quite clear that proof of Christian piety is in works of love done to others, a teaching that (as Weber might say) "is grotesquely at variance" with Weber's own thesis that Calvinists' only proof of piety was to be found in earned wealth' (p. 31). Taken as a whole, Blanchard's interpretation of Calvin, alongside her rereading of Smith, and Chicago School Economics, reaches a number of conclusions. First, that the spirit of capitalism may not be blamed on

Protestantism; that neither may it be legitimised through a close reading of Adam Smith or reduced to the rampant self-interest of Chicago School economists. Ultimately, Blanchard concludes that Capitalism still offers the potential to manifest values of Christian freedom—even while she enjoins Christians to recognise that American capitalism has extensive excesses to apologise for.

Like Blanchard's work, Michael Novak's (1982) *The Spirit of Democratic Capitalism* is also written from an explicitly Christian perspective. Unlike Blanchard, however, Novak's position is that capitalism absolutely owes no apology. Focussing upon American capitalism, Novak argues that 'No society in the long history of the Jewish and Christian people owes more than our own to the inspiration of Jewish, Christian, and humanistic traditions' (p. 21). For Novak, American capitalism is both practically and theologically the best of all known systems of political economy (p. 28). The problem as Novak sees it, however, is that through familiarity, the 'bias' of critics (p. 242) and mistaken criticisms by the Catholic Church, people have forgotten just how beneficent the 'living spirit' of American capitalism is. Novak's book then attempts to rearticulate that living-but-forgotten spirit of American capitalism by providing it with a new theological legitimation. For example, we are told that Judaism and Christianity endorse the idea that human life is a competition and that Christian conceptions of human dignity therefore require that this competition results in inequality (p. 435). Drawing upon his argument in this 1982 work that 'American democratic capitalism has some new things to add to the Catholic tradition' (p. 249), Novak's later work (1993) *The Catholic Ethic and the Spirit of Capitalism* highlights what he argues to have been the Catholic Church's misguided criticisms and applauds Pope John Paul II's realignment of Catholicism with capitalism.

Written from a notably less pro-capitalist position, Luc Boltanski and Eve Chiapello's (1999/2005) *Le Nouvel Esprit du Capitalisme/The New Spirit of Capitalism* has been responsible for considerable reengagement with the spirit of capitalism in both popular and academic arenas. Seeking to explain how capitalist society survives and even thrives from the criticism it generates, the authors argue that the ideological legitimation of capitalism—its spirit—has changed so as to incorporate such critique. Considering the May 1968 protests in France as the symbolic high point of the critique of the homogenising, alienating and impoverishing effects of mid-twentieth-century capitalism, Boltanski and Chiapello argue that capitalism birthed a new spirit. At least as far as the experience of the working elite were concerned, capitalism transformed itself to offer working lives promising creativity, empowerment, variety, individuality, even authenticity. This was accompanied and affected by the widespread dissemination of new management and leadership discourse, which constructed managerial work around concepts such as ethics, charisma, vision, mission and transformative futures. This then enabled the managerial elite to conceive of themselves not as bureaucratic functionaries, but rather as heroic subjects bringing into being a new, bold and necessary future. As with Weber's original work, Boltanski and Chiapello's thesis is not uncontested. Bernard Stiegler's (2006[2014]) *The Lost Spirit of Capitalism*, for example, disputes that capitalism has any such motivational spirit remaining, positing instead that we are witnessing its long but inexorable demise.

> Capitalism has lost its spirit: spiritual misery reigns. Control societies have become uncontrollable, profoundly irrational, without reason, unable to inspire hope. Those who no longer believe they have anything whatsoever to expect from the development of hyperindustrial capitalism are increasingly numerous.
>
> (p. 1)

Within organisational studies, Boltanski and Chiapello's *New Spirit* work has received considerable attention, if a somewhat mixed reception. Paul Du Gay and Glenn Morgan's (2013) edited collection of responses to the text illustrates this well. Contributions to this work range from those seeking to apply elements of Boltanski and Chiapello's analysis to new empirical sites—including financial markets, welfare systems, social movement organisations, higher education and authentic workplaces—to highly critical works which argue that Boltanski and Chiapello have produced an arrogant, totalising text, containing a politically damaging, fatalistic message (Parker 2013), and that they have fundamentally misunderstood Weber's solution to the riddle of capitalism's mobilising spirit (Willmott 2013)—a point I shall return to in the *Conclusion* to this book.

As even this brief overview of a small collection of works shows then, despite it being over a hundred years since Weber's work was first published, the idea of a spirit, or spirits, of capitalism still haunts our imagination. While this might make my own interest in spirit somewhat understandable, it does beg the question as to what yet another spirit text might hope to add that is novel, interesting or hasn't already been said. My way of starting to answer this is to consider what Weber's original work and each of the above, either through argument or omission, seem to assume. This is the assumption that while capitalism's origins may have been steeped in the religious, this has long since been relegated to the far and distant past: the assumption that 'victorious capitalism . . . needs its support no longer' (Weber 1930[2001:124]), such that capitalism today (notwithstanding Novak's wish to make it otherwise) is inexorably secular. But is it?

## Secularism, American Religious Belief and Neoliberalism

Assuming that the capitalist present is inexorably secular puts us in good company. As Gorski et al. (2012:6) observe, '(t)hroughout the twentieth century, the "dominant paradigm" in the social scientific study of religion was secularization theory'. Prevailing social scientific beliefs revolved around the understanding that modernisation undermines religion; that the light of reason—or from a more critical perspective the suffocating hand of instrumental rationality (see Chapter 5 *The Individual*)—would replace religious belief; that the world was inevitably becoming disenchanted and demagified; that public and state office would be increasingly divorced from what was assumed to be waning, privatised, religious sentiment; and that a 'secular' West 'represents the cutting edge of social progress which the rest of the world will follow' (Gaulthier, Martikainen and Woodhead 2013:2). Organisational scholarship too would seem to have subscribed to this dominant secularisation paradigm: exhibiting an 'unreflexively secular metaphysics' and demonstrating 'a long term tendency . . . to see other-worldly or metaphysical beliefs as theoretically insignificant' (Bell and Taylor 2016:552). Shifting from those who would understand the contemporary world to those who would create it, the architects of neoliberalism also conceived of their transformation of contemporary capitalism as a secularised project. Hayek (1967), for example, would cast neoliberalism as the progeny of enlightenment reason, scientific-economic rationality and an irreligious evolutionary theory (Hayek 1967: see Chapter 3 *Devils*). And not just amongst its legislators, amongst its interpreters too the 'prevailing narrative of neoliberalism has foregrounded the importance of secular economic scholars, concepts and justifications for its rise' (Hackworth 2013:93).

This secular interpretation and treatment of neoliberal capitalism is rather contestable however. As Hackworth (2013:95) observes, 'while there certainly are valid reasons for using a secular economic lens to understand neoliberalism's rise as an intellectual project, such an approach falls considerably short of explaining why the idea has political salience'. An important part of the explanation for neoliberalism's political appeal for Hackworth lies in the 'ways in which various radical right Christian philosophical movements support neoliberalism . . . in an ideational way' (ibid). Similarly, for Moreton (2010:5), 'free-market economic theories captured the hearts and minds of elite policymakers in the later twentieth century', however, 'the animating spirit of Christian free enterprise shaped the outcome'. We can start to get some sense of the ongoing significance of the non-secular spirits swirling around the neoliberal present, if we look at the site of Weber's analysis, the spiritual home of neoliberalism and principle source of managerial, organisational and leadership orthodoxy: America.

The well-regarded Pew 'National Religious Landscape Survey Report' (2015) observes that American's belief in the existence of God is 'remarkably high by comparison with other advanced industrial countries' (Pew 2015:3), standing at 89% of the population, with 63% expressing 'absolute certainty' in the existence of God, rising to approximately 90%

certainty amongst the dominant Protestant population. This represented some 'modest reduction' in overall rates of belief since the previous 2008 survey, notwithstanding that 'by some measures, religiously affiliated people appear to have grown *more* religiously observant in recent years' (p. 6). Despite this modest reduction in overall rates of belief, the US is 'perhaps the least secular country in the West' (Gorski et al. 2012:7). Indeed, 'one of the reasons that the secularization thesis has come to seem so dubious is the "anomalous" status of the United States, a clear outlier by most metrics' (ibid:7). However, while from a European perspective—specifically a Western European, and more specifically still, what Taylor (2007:522) calls an 'educated, cultivated' Western European perspective—the US looks like an outlier in terms of the extent and depth of religious belief; when looked at globally, it is Western Europe that is the outlier. The rest of the world is, as Peter Berger (1999:2) has observed, 'just as furiously religious as it ever was, and in some places more so than ever'.

Returning to the Pew survey of the American religious landscape, of the total US population 71% are Christian, of which two thirds are Protestant, with the largest denomination being evangelical protestant (25% of the US population according to the Pew (2015) report; 34% according to a different national survey, see Kosmin and Keysar 2009). Of the US population, 55% pray at least daily and 58% believe scripture to be the word of God. Amongst the Christian population, three quarters believe scripture is the word of God, and amongst the evangelical, Mormon and Jehovah Witnesses denominations approximately 90% do (p. 57). Of the total US population, 72% believe in heaven, 58% believe in hell and 59% believe that human beings have either evolved according to God's design or have always existed in our current form. Again, these figures differ with particular religious affiliations, with 88% of evangelic Christians believing in heaven, 82% in hell and 82% believing that humans either evolved according to God's design or have always existed in their current form. The previous 2008 Pew survey also gathered data regarding the percentage of Americans who believe in miracles occurring today (79%) and in angels and demons existing and being active in the modern world (68%).

Further, religion is not just a matter of private belief—notwithstanding the official constitutional separation of religion from public life in the US. Both the 2008 and 2015 Pew reports find a strong relationship between religious belief, political ideology and affiliation, and social/cultural views. Again, compared with other Western developed nations, the United States has by far the strongest connections between an individual's religious beliefs, their politics and their morals (Norris and Inglehart 2004; Olson 2007). Church attendance 'is now more important in determining voting patterns than gender, income, region or age and is equally as important as race' (Ashley and Sandefer 2013:110). Of the religious faiths and denominations, Mormons and evangelical Christians tend to be the most conservative in their political ideology. The latter are the largest religious group in the Republican Party (Pew 2015), and there is an ongoing trend towards 'more conservative beliefs and particularly to a more "evangelical" outlook among Christians' (Kosmin and Keysar 2009:6).

The relationship of religion and the political in America today is not a case of two hermitically sealed worlds simply coinciding either. Where Charles Taylor (2007), in his well-regarded *A Secular Age*, observed that post-war America's 'tight interweaving' of family, religion, patriotism, sexual mores, and the state was 'roundly repudiated' by the turbulence and developments of the 1960s, the resurgence and reinvention of the economic and Christian American right since the 1980s can be understood to have redrawn this picture again. Whether it has been because of political expediency, a matter of faith or a shared zeitgeist, the US demonstrates 'an apparently smooth alliance between neoliberals and religious fundamentalists' (Hackworth 2013:93). An important manifestation of this alliance is drawn around a shared strong commitment to the dismantling of the welfare state, coupled with a significant redistribution of resources and service provision from the public sector to faith-based, principally Christian, organisations (Ashley and Sandefer 2013; Hackworth 2013; Martikainen 2013). Evangelical Christians have demonstrated a long-held opposition to state remediation of economic inequality, stretching back as far as the era of classical liberalism in the eighteenth century, with poverty variously understood as God's punishment for Original Sin, as revenge against non-believers and as prophesying the end times (Hackworth 2013). Drawing upon this ideological-theological history, by the 1990s the religious right was 'beginning to build elaborate arguments around the assertion that the Bible actually lays out a template for a government without welfare and an economy without regulation' (ibid:98). As Kaplan (2004:72) has observed, the 'conservative economic agenda of lower taxes, deregulation, and downsizing government seemed perfectly tailored to fundamentalist Christians . . . the evangelical movement emphasized personal responsibility, through the life-changing experience of being born again'. For Ashley and Sandefer (2013), we are witnessing a concerted redrawing of the relationship between religion and the state in the US, such that the Christian religion is once again providing a key legitimising discourse that the lifeworld under neoliberalism no longer delivers. Such, indeed, is the affinity between the conservative right and the Christian right in America that Hackworth suggests we use the term 'religious neoliberalism', 'both in the sense that there is a widespread devotion, almost a religious one, to neoliberalism but also, less obviously (but more importantly), the Religious Right has been crucial for providing political support for neoliberal policies' (Hackworth 2013:93).

It is not just at the level of the state or in the realm of politics where we can find a concertedly non-secular spirit providing support for neoliberalism. Bethany Moreton's excellent (2009) *To Serve God and Wal-Mart:*

*The Making of Christian Free Enterprise*, for example, charts myriad connections between free-market business, neoliberal ideology and conservative Christianity—and it is worth quoting at length:

> The University of Chicago and the American Enterprise Institute could not by themselves sustain Milton Friedman's free-market utopia. Rather the popular faith in Christian free enterprise attracted passionate support among many ordinary people. It was nurtured not only on the high planes of elite academe or in the hot-houses of well-funded think tanks, but also in the cultural apparatus of Sun Belt service economy: discount stores, back offices, Christian Business Schools, missionary manuals, Wednesday night Bible study. It was not a simple matter of elite manipulation; it did not make political dupes of Kansans or Arkansans. Rather, for many in the nation's old agricultural periphery, the gospel of free enterprise answered some of their most pressing needs. It compensated for the loss of the yeoman dream of self-sufficiency; it sanctified mass consumption; it raised degraded service labour to the status of a calling; it offered a new basis for family stability and masculine authority even as the logic of the market undermined both; for some whites it eased the dismantling of official white supremacy. The generation that moved from the farm to the store, and the children who filled marketing classes and offices, crafted an ideology of Christian free enterprise from their experience of a particular historical moment, a particular geography, and a particular religious ecology.
>
> (p. 271)

Accompanying, responding to and fuelling the connections between Christianity and the free-market are a plethora of texts and discourses which draw upon non-secular ideas and concepts to further legitimise work, management and leadership under neoliberalism. These range from texts which draw explicitly and unapologetically upon Christianity (for example, Stephens 2016 *Think Like Jesus: A Five Week Devotional for Lady Bosses*; Anderson and Maxwell 2009 *How to Run Your Business by the Book: A Biblical Blueprint to Bless Your Business*; Jones 1996 *Jesus CEO: Using Ancient Wisdom for Visionary Leadership*; Cardone 2009 *Business with Soul: Creating a Workplace Rich in Faith and Values*, see Chapters 2 *Gods* and 4 *Soul*) to those in which the theological ideas and concepts are diffused into the putatively secular business and academic mainstream (for example, theories of Charismatic, Servant, and Spiritual Leadership, discourses of organisational 'vision' and 'mission', and ideas of individual and corporate sovereignty, see Chapter 2 *Gods*; the deification and demonisation of CEOs, notions of corporate 'good' and 'evil', see Chapter 3 *Devils*; and the concepts of corporate social responsibility, business ethics, corporate citizenship and organisational soul, see Chapter 4 *Soul*).

Taking all of the above developments together—the extent and nature of religious belief in America, and worldwide; the strong intersection of religious and political values; the important support of Christian free enterprise for the neoliberal project; the explicitly Christian business texts; and the theologically inflected academic leadership and management works—the idea of inexorable, modernising secularisation

> looks more like a partisan political program than a 'value-free' social theory. The view that reason would replace religion and, more fundamentally, that reason is opposed to religion—the conventional wisdom among right-thinking intellectuals just a generation ago—is now being called into question. Perhaps it was the secularists rather than the religionists who were blinded, not by the darkness, but by *les lumières* of Enlightenment reason. While many assumed that religion was an ailing patient in the back wards of historical development, it was engaged in a worldwide revival tour.
>
> (Gorski et al. 2012:6)

As Moreton (2010:87) writes, with specific reference to Weber's thesis of desacralised American capitalism, '(t)he political impact of the New Christian Right in the 1980s forced a reappraisal of this narrative'.

## The Structure and Spirit of This Book

Except, it hasn't. Or at least it hasn't forced such a reappraisal very widely yet amongst scholars of work and organisation. For while there have been calls for organisational scholars to 'take religion seriously' (Tracey, Phillips and Lounsbury 2014), for a 'theology of organisation' (Sørensen et al. 2012) and for social science to better engage with the postsecular (McLellan 2007), sustained engagement with the ways the non-secular intersects with work organisations in neoliberalism has not been a significant focus of organisation studies to date. This book then is an attempt to contribute towards remedying this, by offering a critical examination of religious ideas, concepts and invocations—what I'm calling *spirits*—that are haunting, speaking to and supporting business in the neoliberal present. It is structured into four chapters (plus this *Introduction* and a *Conclusion*) organised respectively around the concepts of *Gods*, *Devils*, *Soul* and *The Individual*.

Chapter 2, '*Gods*', examines the neoliberal elevation of business leadership to an omnipotent status. Drawing upon research that demonstrates that the return in the US to pre-1930 levels of inequality is fed largely by upper management remuneration, I show how such political might is accorded an ethical warrant, a warrant which dovetails with the long-observed romanticised, mythologised conceptualisation of leadership. I chart a variety of significant constructions in the West's ideals of ethical sovereignty and show how these are employed in the legitimation of business leaders' status. These include the Enlightenment man of reason, Romantic authenticity, Feudal relationships of patronage and privilege and, central for the focus of this text, ideas of religiosity and deification. I examine the evocation of religion in leadership discourse, both in the large volume of explicitly Christian texts aimed at business leaders and in the putatively secular Spiritual Leadership and Servant Leadership theories. I end by highlighting some consequences of our sanctification of business leaders, including the historical sins of idolatry and hubris.

Continuing the theme of examining sins, Chapter 3, 'Devils', considers the nature of evil as it applies to critiques of capitalism. I start by documenting the use of the Devil, since the early modern period, to critique capitalism and show the continuation of this thematic in popular media critiques of corporate malfeasance and CEOs who have spectacularly fallen from grace. Having shown the historic, and continual, use of demonisation to criticise capitalism and its agents, the chapter considers the ideas of evil and the devil across a number of religious, philosophical and literary texts. I consider distinctions between natural and moral evils, theodical justifications of evil both ancient and modern, and conceptualisations of radical versus banal evil. I use these ideas to reread neoliberal corporate practices including those of outsourcing, tax avoidance, climate change denial and the pursuit of corporate sovereignty.

If certain corporate practices may be considered as evils, perhaps we need corporations that are governed with soul? Chapter 4, 'Soul', considers this idea, starting by highlighting how ideas of 'organisational soul' are used in popular management texts to celebrate corporations that are governed through the beliefs of their leaders. Problematising the celebratory co-optation of soul in these texts, I re-examine soul through a number of texts and traditions in the West's long religio-philosophical engagement. These include Aurelius Augustine's first hermeneutics of the subject, key constitutive moral practices of Late Antiquity and Early Christianity, Classical Greek philosophy, writings on governmentality and Weber and Hegel's articulation of a trans- or supra-human spirit/*geist*. Applying these sources to contemporary discussions of the citizenship or subject status of the corporation, I consider whether we may understand neoliberal corporations to have souls, what kinds of souls they may have and how we may seek to discipline them—as we have come to understand human souls to be disciplined—through processes of governmentality.

If we can't rely on the spontaneous goodness of contrite corporate souls or the beneficence of sovereign leaders, perhaps our focus needs to move to individual organisational members? Chapter 5, 'The Individual', begins by showing how an appeal to the category of the individual has been fundamental to liberal and neoliberal thought: running through the work of John Locke, the philosophers and legislators of the French Revolution, and classical liberalism and neoliberal tracts. Lock step with this, I show

how criticisms of the category of the individual raged across such sources as the Victorian novel, the writings of grand Victorian critic Karl Marx, and were continued in twentieth-century Critical Theory, industrial sociology and late twentieth-century continental philosophy, culminating, perhaps, with Levinas' radical destabilising of the individual self as the basis of ethics. Not giving up on the individual just yet, I draw out the category's religious roots and 2000-year construction and consider whether, by attending to its formative theological beginnings, we may yet reconceptualise the individual in a manner more able to reconcile ethics, the self and others in a way which avoids both sovereignty and subjugation.

Throughout my engagement with the above material, I am seeking to do three broad things in this book. First, I wish to show how theologically resonant concepts are being deployed in current managerial, leadership and organisation discourses. Second, I am seeking to unearth, dust off, and examine religio-historical and philosophical roots of these concepts. And third, through critical reappraisal and reengagement, I am seeking to demonstrate how the religio-historical and religio-philosophical can be brought into the lexicon of critical organisational scholarship—with the hope that by so doing we may better engage, critique and reframe non-secular legitimations of neoliberalism and its institutions. As the above chapter summaries might suggest, in doing the above this book draws upon a transdisciplinary combination of texts and sources. These variously include contemporary, modern and ancient philosophy; religio-historical and theological sources; classic and modern literary works; business texts and practices; research in the field of organisational studies; and contemporary social theory. If nothing else, I hope that the consciously eclectic assortment of texts and ideas that constitute this book might make for an interesting read.

There are two final points that I'd like to make to end this introduction. In my engagement with the religious spirits swirling through and around neoliberalism, I have limited myself principally to discussing Christian religious sources and their influences. I have done so for a number of reasons: because this maps onto Weber's original concentration upon Christianity in *The Protestant Ethic and the Spirit of Capitalism*; because the Christian faith—particularly its evangelical arm—is proving especially influential in legitimising and mobilising neoliberalism in its US heartland; and because, while I am not a believer myself, by virtue of my own cultural heritage Christianity is the religion which I feel least unqualified to discuss.

Finally, combining my abiding academic interest in ethics with the fact that for the last two millennia the Christian religion has been intimately tied to constructions of who, and what, 'we' as Western subjects *are*, I use this book also to engage with questions of ethical subjectivity. In particular I consider whether consideration of our formative historico-religious foundations might help us to reconceptualise the nature of the ethical subject and its relationship to others and to organisation. So, to this end, in *Gods* I examine the idea of 'sovereignty' and 'sovereign individuality', highlighting this as the problematic core of the discourse of leadership and the deification of the CEO. In *Devils* I show how the search for sovereignty has long been understood as a manifestation of evil—even as the *original* evil—and I explore contemporary corporate practices in these terms. In *Soul* I examine the category favoured by critical organisational scholars—'the subject'—showing how this category contests the idea of ethical sovereignty, but arguing that it does so while risking reproducing ethics as wholly *subject to* politics and power. Finally, in *The Individual*, I draw upon founding theological conceptualisations of the self to present ethical subjectivity neither as sovereign nor wholly subject to, but rather as a form of *plural individuality* in which the other is always, already, part of the self.

# 2 Gods

> . . . they anxiously conjure up the spirits of the past to their service, borrowing from them names, battle slogans, and costumes in order to present this new scene in world history in time-honoured disguise and borrowed language.
>
> Karl Marx (1852), *The Eighteenth Brumaire of Louis Bonaparte*

> . . . the political concept of rank always transforms itself into a spiritual concept of rank.
>
> Friedrich Nietzsche (1887[1996]:17, *On the Genealogy of Morals: A Polemic.* (© Douglas Smith, translator and editor. By permission of Oxford University Press)

On January 20th, 2017, a celebrity business leader, with no governmental, military or legislative experience, was elevated to the position of President of the United States of America, the superpower with the world's largest nuclear arsenal. He proceeded to install other business leaders into key positions in his administration, including Secretary to the Treasury, Secretary of Commerce, Secretary of Labour, Secretary of State, Head of Small Business Administration and Special Advisor on Regulatory Reform. The message was that we should trust business leaders to 'Make America Great Again'.

In a heavily cited article, Pfeffer (1977) argued that the figure of the business leader had become a repository of our hopes, aspirations, anxieties and desires. Donald Trump's election and appointments suggest that Pfeffer's analysis is truer today than ever. Where Alistair MacIntyre (1985) considered the manager to be the central moral subject of the 1980s, the business leader can justifiably be regarded as occupying that space now. It is a figure that carries quite different meanings to the managerial qualities of procedural calculation, technical rationality and presumed moral neutrality that MacIntyre identified. No neutral functionary, the business leader compounds the authority of office with an older, charismatic, power. Their job is to inspire, enthral or seduce (Calàs and Smircich 1991) followers. Leadership has a 'highly romanticised', 'mythological' status 'that exceeds the limits of normal scientific inquiry' (Meindl, Ehrlich and Dukerich 1985:78). Leaders 'must be endowed with superhuman qualities because only then can they really be perceived as real leaders, accepted and respected' (Gabriel 1997:338–339). Far more than mere rules or policy to follow, the leader is to provide values, mission, vision and ethics for the organisation. Embodying not just the ethos of bureaucracy or even the ethics of a narrow instrumental capitalism, business leaders are paragons of moral character, courage and virtue. Business leaders have become the living embodiment of the organisation, its values, culture and morals. Jack Walsh *was* General Electric; Steve Jobs *was* Apple; Richard Branson *is* Virgin. As Robert's (2001:118) writes,

> [a]t least within the imagined boundary of the corporation, in their perfection, these individuals have as it were walked through the mirror in which they now hold others to account. In becoming the boss they become *the subject:* the ones who determine and are not themselves determined. Arguably then they are the ones at most risk of coming to believe themselves to be essentially sovereign and autonomous.

This sovereignty has been crowned through the deregulation of capital, tightening regulation on labour and the mobility of the transnational corporation. The business leader is at the top of the hierarchy—where the concept of hierarchy itself originated in relation to divinity, in the ordering and ranking of angels in their upward-looking relationship to God (Parker 2009). The leader's celestial light trickles down, as wealth is supposed to also, and followers are encouraged and expected to ever reflect back the leader's haloed status (Parker 2009; Kets de Vries 1991). Fantasies of divine grace expand beyond the narcissistic preoccupations of the leader to form part of the psychological backdrop of organisational members. Thus meeting the leader may come to acquire the psychological import of 'the archetypal Christian scene of meeting God as supreme ruler on the day of judgement' (Gabriel 1997:316), a dynamic which continues 'the long conventional representation of leaders as saints or Gods' (Grint 2010:90), and evokes Nietzsche's observation from the start of this chapter.

How is it though that business leadership, something which on the surface might be understood as little more than an obfuscation of prosaic management, has become intertwined with images of unfettered sovereignty, even divinity? For one really quite convincing answer to this question we might proffer a straightforward historical materialist reading, drawing upon Marx and Engel's (1845[1932]) observation that the 'ruling ideas are nothing more than the ideal expression of the dominant material relationships, the dominant material relationships grasped as ideas'. Thus we could simply see this elevation of the leadership of corporations to a sacralised sovereignty as a manifestation of the inequalities of neoliberal societies. And there is indeed ample evidence to show how business leaders' salaries, shares and bonuses have enabled them to achieve an economic position of such fantastical magnitude that it might be seen to require a celestial justification. As a 2017 *Oxfam* report documented, eight businessmen now own the same amount of wealth as the poorest half of the world (3.6 billion people), each FTSE-100 CEO earns as much in a year as 10,000 people working in garment factories in Bangladesh, and the world's 10 biggest corporations together have revenue greater than that of the combined government revenue of 180 of the world's 195 countries. According to a *Business Week* report (cited in Flanagan 2003), the average US CEO made a healthy 42 times the average US employee's wage in 1980. By 1990 it was 85 times. By 2000, the average CEO was paid a staggering 531 times the average employee wage—these figures also did not include the lucrative share options that CEO are awarded. And in 2018, new Securities and Exchange Commission rules provided us with data about an individual corporation's actual (rather than national average) CEO-to-employee wage differentials: from this we learnt that CEO of Yum brands (which owns Pizza Hut, KFC and Taco Bell) made 1358 times more than the company's average employee; CEO of VF Corporation (which owns Lee, North Face, Timberland and Vans) made 1353 times; and CEO of toy maker Mattel makes 4987 times what their average employee makes (Stewart 2018). Unsurprisingly, given the above, inequality has skyrocketed since the advent of neoliberalism, such that the richest 1% of the world's population has, since 2015, owned more wealth than the remaining 99% of the planet (*Oxfam* 2017). Thomas Picketty has shown how, in the US, inequality has now returned to the 'quantitatively extreme' (2017:367) peak last seen at the end of the Victorian era. What is more, this extreme inequality is 'largely the result of an unprecedented increase in wage inequality and in particular the emergence of extremely high remunerations at the summit of the wage hierarchy, particularly among top managers of large firms' (ibid:374). '(W)hat primarily characterizes the United States at the moment is a record level of inequality of income from labour . . . probably higher than in any other society at any time in the past, anywhere in the world' (ibid:332). Both in the US and the other English-speaking countries, 'the primary reason for increased income inequalities in recent decades is the rise of the supermanager in both financial and non-financial sectors' (ibid:398). In sum, the 'spectacular increase in inequality largely reflects an unprecedented explosion of very elevated incomes from labour, a veritable separation of the top managers of large firms from the rest of the population' (ibid:32).

Explaining leadership's sovereignty and sacralisation (Grint 2010) as the simple exercise of power that the unprecedented economic elevation of the 'supermanagers' (Picketty 2017) accords them is, unsurprisingly, not the construction favoured by modern societies which still rely upon harnessing the discretionary effort of formally voluntary labour. Instead, leadership is socially constructed (Fairhurst and Grant 2010) in a variety of other ways which seek to excuse and explain its sovereignty. Thus, while the appropriation and transference of money may go a long way towards explaining the bare fact of the sacralisation of leadership, if we want to understand some of the considerable variety in the form that constructions and articulations of leadership take then we also need to do something more genealogical in style. That is, we need to examine how a particular subject-position—the 'business leader'—is constituted through prior discourses, assumptions, practices and the like. And in so doing, to examine the 'central interaction between belief systems and inequality regimes' (Picketty 2017:545) to expose how the subject of leadership is enmeshed in antecedent forms of power and implicitly evoked natural orders (Gordon's 2010). That is, we need to conduct an analysis which is attuned to the ways that the remarkably elevated sovereign subject position of the 'business leader' is formed from an uneasy amalgam of 'what went before'.

## The Construction of Sovereign Individuality

What went before is a broader historical and philosophical context in which the idea of sovereignty in the West unfolds. Since at least the emergence of Christianity in the fading days of the Roman empire, this unfolding takes place through arrogations of sovereignty—from God, to the Church and Royalty, to the (liberal) State and certain of its citizens, and latterly to the neoliberal corporation and its 'leadership'.

Starting with one of the West's origin tales, patronised tenants Adam and Eve learn the attributes of bad conscience only once they appropriate the forbidden property of the 'tree of knowledge of good and evil'. They are cast out of Eden and cursed with a newfound moral culpability, that stain of sin which will follow their descendants for eternity. Though outcast they are still strictly subject to God's prohibitions, judgements and commandments, with their descendants having to undergo a recurring series of trials (Abraham), punishments (Sodom) and holocausts (the Great Flood) for offending against His morality. In this origin tale sovereignty vests with God, the moral agency of humankind is reduced to a binary choice: obedience or damnation.

Under conditions of Feudalism, prevailing in Europe from around the eleventh century onwards, the Church and monarchy's monopolistic ownership of productive property (*land*, in this still predominantly agrarian society) is supported by Christian religious doctrine which assigns duties and obligations to each stratum of society. Lords of the manor, as custodians rather than owners of the land, have both paternalistic and charitable duties as guardians of the peasantry who work the land. In turn, the peasantry have duties of loyalty and obligation to the lord and are obliged to 'a fundamental respect for existing arrangements' (O'Flynn 2009:9).

These reciprocal though fundamentally uneven relationships constitute the moral basis of society, replicating in the earthly realm the paternal relationship of the Christian God with his children. The sovereignty of the landed classes is here considerable but constrained, obligations of guardianship and paternalism remain and, of the peasants, it is minimal, tightly limited within strict duties of loyalty.

The emergence of moveable capital and the acquisitive, accumulative behaviour which this enabled challenged prevailing Feudal moralities. Acquisitive behaviour was sinful under the Church's teaching of avarice and usury. Moral obligations tying the control of land capital with paternalistic guardianship and charity were restrictive of continuous capital accumulation. Customary obligations of loyalty and duty to the lord and land were not supportive of the new relationships of labour called upon by the emerging bourgeoisie. The emergence of capitalist society was accompanied and supported therefore by concurrent developments of new moralities founded upon the ideal of the individual (O'Flynn 2009). In the sphere of religion, as Weber (1930[2001]) observes, the Protestant Reformation was instrumental in the development of the kind of individualised moral subjectivity necessary for the birth of capitalism. Protestantism, particularly the tradition of Calvinism, redrew the relationship between God, the Church and the population, eliminating the securing of salvation through obedience to Church and performing of sacraments (p. 61). Protesting the Catholic Church's monopolistic claim to arbitrate the future of the soul, '(t)he Calvinist's intercourse with his God was carried on in deep spiritual isolation' (p. 63), placing 'the individual entirely on his own responsibility in religious matters' (p. 65) and ushering in the wider tendency to 'tear the individual away from the closed ties with which he is bound to this world' (p. 64). This privileging of individual conscience and individualised responsibility is subsequently drawn upon by a figure such as John Locke, himself originally a Calvinist, in his crafting of what came to be understood as the philosophical foundation of liberalism. Locke's (1690[1980]) *Second Treatise on Government* squared God's provision of the world in common with a sacrosanct moral right for an individual to appropriate parts of that world as private property once 'he hath mixed his labour with, and joined to it something that is his own' (p. 19). 'Industrious and rational' (p. 21) individuals, who used their labour power to organise and employ other less industrious people, could also rightly claim the latter's labour as their own. Thus, 'the turfs my servant has cut; and the one I have digged . . . become my property' (pp. 19–20). This commoditisation of labour and its appropriation as the private property of the employer are legitimised as natural, universal and, indeed, willed by God. The central subject of the emerging capitalist society represents then a fundamental departure from the Feudal ideals of reciprocal moral obligations through guardianship, duty, obligation or charity. As Marx observed, '[t]he right to private property is therefore the right to enjoy and dispose of one's resources as one wills, without regard for other men and independently of society: the right of self interest' (Marx 1843[2012]:23). Though formally universal, through its foundational intersection with property Locke's sovereign subject status is unevenly distributed. Thus, for instance, the right to vote in elections in Locke's political philosophy—and the West's history—was restricted to male subjects of the independently propertied class.

Such uneven translation of a formally universal precept is carried through into the unfolding of the sovereign subject in that 'age of reason', the Enlightenment. Founded upon a philosophical privileging of *man*kind's capacity to reason as the basis of freedom from external and traditional authority, ethics and morality too was to be progressively liberated from the bounds of religious revelation and subjected to reason. Thus, in the moral theories of so central a figure of the Enlightenment, Kant, and in the strongly contrasting calculative utilitarian ethics of those such as Bentham, the capacity for reason serves as the basis of ethics. Though formally universal, the privileging of reason as an abstract and distancing mode of thought served, as Benhabib (1992) has argued, to elevate interactions in the public realm between independent, property-owning, male heads of households to the status of 'justice' and 'ethics' while relegating interpersonal relations and emotions to the domestic, intimate sphere. 'An entire domain of human activity', writes Benhabib, 'namely, nurture, reproduction, love and care, which becomes the woman's lot in the course of the development of modern bourgeois society is excluded from moral and political considerations, and relegated to the realm of "nature"' (p. 276). The Enlightenment's rationalisation of nature and the emotions was challenged early by the Romantic era. Romanticism, as a reaction to the privileging of reason and industry, promoted the direct experience of sublime nature and valorised the psyche, authenticity and intuition—most particularly of the artist. Still fundamentally individualistic—privileging ideals of heroism, direct individual experience and the authenticity of the inner self—Romanticism nevertheless critiqued the narrow rationality and scientific reductionism of the Enlightenment. As such, Romanticism's contribution 'to something like the melting away of the very notion of objective truth' (Berlin 1990:57) may be understood to have anticipated some of the later contributions of Continental Philosophy—a mode of theorising the social which combined a Romantic-inspired critique of Enlightenment rationality with an original, profound, conceptual challenge to the ideal of an integrated, independent, sovereign self. Notwithstanding this conceptual challenge to the sovereign individual, or indeed those periods where formulations of politics in the West sought to collectivise individuals' fates through a greater attentiveness to the communal (communism, socialism and the like), the modern history of the West has been written from the position of a culture enmeshed within dreams of property-based sovereignty and individualism—however poorly such dreams are realised in reality.

Ensuring and enshrining the liberty of the sovereign, property-owning individual came to be understood as best undertaken by a liberal government. As Locke (1690[1980]) argued, 'the great and chief end . . . of men's uniting into commonwealths, and putting themselves under government, is the preservation of their property' (p. 66) thus 'the preservation of property being the end of government, and that for which men enter society' (p. 73). Liberalism's conflation of liberty with private property was later directly carried into neoliberalism, articulated as a central thesis of Friedman's (1962) *Capitalism and Freedom* and Hayek's (1960) *The Constitution of Liberty*. The foundation statement of the influential Mont Pelerin Society, in which these two figures were central, illustrates this well:

> The central values of civilization are in danger. Over large stretches of the earth's surface the essential conditions of human dignity and freedom have already disappeared . . . these developments have been fostered . . . by a decline of belief in private property and the competitive market; for without the diffused power and initiative associated with these institutions it is difficult to imagine a society in which freedom may be effectively preserved.
>
> (Mont Pelerin Society 1947)

From the above brief tour of the ideal of sovereignty in the West, we can start to say several things about the intersection of sovereignty and leadership today. Most obviously we can say that the elevated sovereignty of the business leader, coming at a time when the business corporation under conditions of neoliberalism has dramatically increased its share of society's wealth, may be understood as continuing a long conflation in the West of the command of wealth and an accorded or assumed sovereign status. We can observe too that this conflation has always been accomplished through the denial of such status to others. Historically these others have been, variously, the peasantry, the poor, women, unenlightened populations and the (non)citizens of 'uncivilized' nations. Latterly, they include the liberal state itself (as neoliberalism continues to contest the state's right to arbitrate and manage the social, parcelling out this 'social responsibility' to the corporation) and the employee (as organisations assume sovereignty over organisational members' 'souls': du Gay and Salaman 1992; Rose 1989; Willmott 1993).

We can also start to see something rather interesting about how the subject of leadership, and the subject who leads, are constructed in academic and popular literatures. Faced with leadership's elevation to apparent sovereignty in contemporary neoliberal society—an elevation likely unpalatable if presented as a mere imposition of material and monetary power—there is a casting around and sifting through this cultural history to find legitimations of leadership's elevated status. Leadership today, as I show in the next section, is represented and conceptualised variously in ways that reproduce the Enlightenment faith in (a masculine) rationality; the Romantic privileging of the authenticity of certain individuals' inner life; the exclusions and occlusions of other subjects that always accompanied Enlightenment philosophy and bourgeois modernity; the Feudal relationships of patrimonial privilege and the obligations of the peasants' duty and obedience; and, of particular interest for the concerns of this book, the ultimate Sovereign's divine rule foundational to the Christian religion.

## Secular Legitimations of Leadership Sovereignty

Of course, in many accounts of leadership nothing as poetic as Kings or Gods are evoked. Rather, leaders and leadership are authorised through more 'business-like' discourses, focusing on such things as the leader's ability to make impartial and effective instrumental–rational decisions in complex contexts. Such accounts and authorisations draw not upon Feudal or divine legitimations but rather upon the idea of reason, a concept central to the period of the Enlightenment when it was used to legitimise emerging individualistic subjectivities that contested Feudal arrangements. Leaders and leadership are authorised in terms of their unique or heightened relationship to reason both directly, in terms of the leader's imputed intellect and heightened capacity for clear and sound judgement, and indirectly, inscribed into technical/rational/scientific expert systems, market analysis, statistical forecasting and the like to which the leader has access. We can see such constructions and legitimations of leadership reproduced in a range of media. For example, they are foundational to the prestigious (pseudo)scientific academic literature on strategy (that higher order abstract thinking so central to the legitimacy claims of leadership), are encoded within the proliferation of expert analytical and decision support systems and software, and are embedded in business schools' penchant for capstone business strategy simulations, where leadership is cast as a distanced, intellectual exercise, a rationalised process of quantitative information analysis and programmable response. More than these specific examples, though, it simply seems to 'stand to reason' that the leaders of large corporate entities are there by warrant of their intellectual abilities and capacity for making rational decisions in the long-term interest of the corporation (that is, if we can quieten those nagging, long-standing observations of the highly ambiguous relationship of leadership to organisational performance, Pfeffer 1977, and the deeply political nature of elite status in organised society, Mills 1956).

Authorising relations of power and inequality through a discourse of reason is far from new in the history of work organisations. In the denied, illegitimate birth of modern management in the slave-worked plantations of America, management asserted both rational and moral authority to legitimise their rule (Cooke 2003). A generation later,

Taylor (1911) privileged reason—a capacity possessed only by managers of the organisation—in his construction of a 'scientific' legitimation for work-intensification, deskilling and managerial control over the labour process. Mayo subsequently constructed management as a rational elite which could ensure commitment and compliance by manipulating the irrational needs of employees (Grint 1995). Such a formulation was reproduced later by Peters and Waterman (1982) and their compatriots in corporate culture. If management is the technical/rational elite, standing apart from the sectional, anti-progressive and/or irrational views of the worker as such accounts would have us believe, then the higher up one is in the hierarchy the further one is from the pull of proximity to the superstitious ways of the ordinary worker and the greater is one's inferred clarity of thought and purpose. The leader, as the very pinnacle of this technical/rational hierarchy, is legitimised in their individuated subject status through an almost absolute claim to such rationality. Authorising leadership through ascribing a heightened or unique capacity to reason to the leader thus extends the longer history of managerial ideologies that have deployed reason and its corollaries (science, rationality, impartiality, objective thought, the capacity to make the hard but necessary decisions, etc.) to authorise a political relationship whereby employees' productive capacity is rendered manageable and appropriable property (Jaffee 2001). Such use of reason to authorise leadership and the privatisation of property replicates the Enlightenment's deployment of the same to legitimise the highly prejudicial sovereignty of some at the expense of others. And, as with that earlier era-defining deployment, the reason that legitimates the business leader is enmeshed within a masculine individualism which privileges relations of separation and distance from others as the basis of the retention of sovereignty. Be it on the top floor, the first-class lounge, behind a veil of impeccable self-control and projected confidence, the growing differentials in reward between the CEO and the 'ordinary' employee, or behind the quantification and abstraction of the organisational lifeworld into stock performance and statistics, separation and distance from others is valorised as the necessary prerequisite for impartial thought and the welcomed perquisite of status and wealth (Bauman 2001; Wray-Bliss 2013).

We can see a further shoring up of the masculine sovereign self, with its defining denial of reliance upon others, in the popular and sizeable genre of CEO (auto)biographies. The de rigueur depiction of the 'self-made man' in these works casts the elite status and privilege of corporate stewardship not as a consequence of relational advantage or communal debt—be this modern class and sex privilege, the old-boy network, inherited wealth and status or the labour of others—but rather as the atomistic product of superior intellect and *single*-minded application. Such strident individualisation carries over Locke's (1690[1980]) earlier legitimation of dominion over others' commoditised labour as the natural right of the 'industrious and rational' (p. 21) man of the Enlightenment. The construction of a radically and unabashed sovereign subjectivity is powerfully displayed too in currently popular attempts to theorise and promote the concept of 'authentic leadership'. Responding to the possibility that charismatic, transformational leaders might exercise their leadership in ways not wholly benign (Bass and Steidlmeier 1999), authentic leadership centres upon the idea that leaders need to look within to their 'true or core self' (Gardner, Avolio and Luthans 2005:345) such that 'the more people remain true to their core values, identities, preferences and emotions, the more authentic they become' (Avolio et al. 2004:802). This inner core of the authentic leader provides a 'moral foundation of legitimate values' (Bass and Steidlmeier 1999:184) and renders authentic leaders 'moral agents, [who] expand the domain of effective freedom, the horizon of conscience and the scope for altruistic intention' (p. 211). By turning their attention within, the authentic and necessarily moral leader is rendered a radically sovereign subject, 'self referential' and 'unencumbered by others' expectations for them' (Avolio and Gardner 2005:320 and 319). In authentic leadership, we see the legitimation of the elevation of leadership not by drawing upon the Enlightenment privileging of reason—the business leader as a rational elite shored up by reference to expert knowledge, science and technology—but rather on the Romantic critique of the Enlightenment. Describing the Romantic period in the West, Berlin argues that 'in the realm of ethics, politics and aesthetics it was the authenticity and sincerity of the pursuit of inner goals that mattered' (Berlin 1990:57). Such authenticity, crucially, came not from reasoned and rational theorising. Rather authenticity was achieved through experientially and emotionally traversing the depths of nature—both external nature and one's own inner nature. Like the authentic business leader, who having found their true self acts now only in moral ways (Ford and Harding 2011), Romantic writers believed that the authentic artist, freed from the artificial confines of convention, would spontaneously follow natural laws of artistic inspiration. Such Romantic thinking is irremediably individualistic—the privilege and power of leadership is legitimised as the consequence of the core, inner self of the individual leader. It is also non-egalitarian. It is not coincidental that Romantic historian Thomas Carlyle (1841), perhaps the first modern writer on leadership (Grint 2011:8), coined and exemplified the phrase 'hero-worship' in his *On Heroes, Hero-Worship and the Heroic in History* (1841): a work which represented social and political events and eras as the outcome of the acts of individual heroic figures. In the Romantic era, the hero was often a flawed, all-to-human character— think Byron for example with his addictions, prurience and premature death. However, our modern authentic leaders, laundered through the positive psychology movement, are reduced to banal goodness. As Ford and Harding observe, '[t]he essential, true self of an authentic leader is inherently good, it would seem' (2011:467). Despite all that we have come to know about the human condition, the unconscious and the deeply political, symbolically and actually violent nature of progression in organised society, there is *de facto* no darkness or shadow side (Kets de Vries and Balazs 2011) within the authentic leader's inner selves. These self-referential, sovereign subjects are quintessentially good.

In other attempts to grapple with the sovereignty of the leader, writers have moved from reason or romanticism to the regal. Feudalism, for example, is evoked in Jackall's (1988) highly influential and widely cited critique of managerial amorality. Jackall presents contemporary US corporations as combining the 'pure form' of rational–legal bureaucracy with a 'quasifeudal', 'patrimonial' bureaucracy, which characterised 'the organizational form of the courts of kings and princes' (p. 11). The modern corporate world is thus defined by manager 'barons' (p. 21), whose freedom not only to run their 'fiefs' and utilise their 'vassals' (p. 22) as they might see fit, but also to experience and express their own values and moralities, is fundamentally subordinated to their 'obligations of fealty' (p. 19) to the 'king' (p. 21) and to avoid at all costs his displeasure. In these neo-Feudal corporations, there is precious little leadership at managerial, even senior managerial, levels because there is precious little sovereignty. Instead, there is only upward-looking obligation, fear, courtly cunning and opportunism. Leadership in these bleak bureaucracies resides entirely with the CEO-King. 'His word is law; even the CEO's wishes and whims are taken as commands by close subordinates on the corporate staff, who turn them into policies and directives' (p. 21). The deployment of the epoch of Feudalism to describe contemporary business, and the kinds of moralities allowed and prohibited there, is not restricted to Jackall. Contemporary capitalism and the role of the corporation within this has been likened to a 'Medieval Replay' (Gramm 1989:367), a 'new feudalism' (Baratz 1970:80), a 'modern form of feudalism' (Saul 1997:94) and a situation in which the 'corporation mimics the (medieval) manor' (Adams 1992:398; also Moon 1995). Building upon such critiques, Schwartz (2000) argues that the ethical leadership embodied in the corporate codification and enforcement of ethical codes is an 'unconscionable regression' to a quasi-Feudalist relationship within which organisational member's moralities are stripped of the free exercise of conscience and reduced to mere compliance 'devoid of ethical content' (p. 173). In these Feudal characterisations of leadership, we thus see another representation that leaves little possibility for ethical agency by other organisational members. Jackall (1988), for example, seems to see only exit as the way that managerial subjects might retain an ethics worthy of the name and for Schwartz (2000), as we have seen, the quasi-Feudal imposition of the organisational ethical code serves only a restrictive function, occluding other's ethical agency. While not necessarily evoking Feudalism explicitly, we can see a similar critique of the *necessarily* non-moral nature of hierarchically imposed ethical codes in much of the self-consciously critical writing on business ethics (Wray-Bliss

2009). For such critics, ethics in the business organisation is not something that can be led or managed by an act of imposition by the sovereign or their representatives. CEOs' attempts to control the ethical conduct of other organisational members from a distance 'depends upon the restriction of local moral sensibility, displacing it with incentives to conform with distant interests, even if these now claim to be ethical interests' (Roberts 2003:259). For such reasons, 'this new regime of ethical business is no ethics at all' (ibid 2001:110). Instead, it represents the height of corporate egoism and the narcissistic preoccupations of a leader so seduced by their own sovereignty that they seek to remake all subjects in their image. This brings us to the considerable range and variety of material which associates business leadership and the divine.

## A Divine Right to Rule

> So, is this a business book? Yes. Is this a self-help book? Yes. Is this an inspirational book? Yes. Simply put, it's a tool to help you to take God out of the spiritual compartment of your private spiritual life and give Him free reign in all your daily actions and relationships, especially your leadership roles. . . . We want you to trust Jesus as your leadership model, so whether you're leading in business, in nonprofit organizations, in your community, or at home, you will make Jesus smile.
>
> (Blanchard and Hodges 2003:11 *Servant Leader*)

Contemporary connections of business leadership with the divine are numerous and varied. Articles in the *Financial Times* (Griffith 1997), *Business Week* (Conlin 1999), *Fortune* (Gunther 2001) and *Chief Executive* (Sherwood 2002) chart the rise of proselytising Christian Chief Executive Officers; Nash (1994) examined the beliefs and practices of over 85 evangelical Christian CEOs and top executives; US-based multinational corporation Tyson Foods Inc. placed 128 part-time, principally evangelical or fundamentalist, chaplains in 78 plants in the United States; and both Tyson Foods and the world's biggest company, Wal-Mart, have been significant financial backers of the US Christian Right (Hedges 2006); Wal-Mart's connections and support for conservative Christianity take a variety of additional forms—and include funding student societies to evangelise the virtues of free enterprise and funding higher educational institutions to develop new generations of Christian business leaders (Moreton 2010). Curricula for Christian business leaders need texts to work with—and for those looking to connect religion with a leadership role a large number of works are available. These include such titles as *Think Like Jesus: A Five Week Devotional for Lady Bosses* (Stephens 2016), *How to Run Your Business by the Book: A Biblical Blueprint to Bless Your Business* (Anderson and Maxwell 2009), *The Leadership Genius of Jesus* (Beausay 2009), *Leadership Lessons of Jesus* (Briner and

Pritchard 2008), *Lead Like Jesus: Lessons from the Greatest Leadership Role Model of All Time* (Blanchard and Hodges 2008), *CEO for God, Family and Country* (Johnson 2006), *The Management Methods of Jesus* (Briner 2005), and *God Is My CEO: Following God's Principles in a Bottom Line World* (Julian 2002). Such works typically combine pop-leadership concepts and a self-help format with quotes from scripture, to present Jesus as an executive leader whose methods can be copied for corporate and personal success. Laurie Beth Jones' best-selling (1996) book, *Jesus CEO: Using Ancient Wisdom for Visionary Leadership*, for example, summarises Jesus' lessons for the business leader of today in 85 homilies. Included amongst these are 'He kept in constant contact with his Boss', 'He formed a team', 'He was a turnaround specialist', 'He clearly defined their work-related benefits', and 'He stuck to his mission'. In this last one we are reminded that:

> In the wilderness Jesus was given several 'business opportunities' that did not relate to his mission. Each of these opportunities was related to talents that Jesus had, and used, in some form or another during his tenure. But he resisted them because they did not fit his mission statement.
>
> (ibid:13)

The benefits for the business leader of today in learning Jesus' leadership lessons are potentially miraculous, as Laurie Beth Jones makes clear in an *Industry Week* interview:

> Jesus was a master at building relationships with people—to the point that they were willing to work for free, even to die for him! What business leader wouldn't love to have a team of workers and fellow managers like that? So I lay out some of the things he did to help build those kinds of relationships.
>
> (Brown 1995:18)

Success is also, according to Jones' unabashed co-option of Christianity's promise, ensured:

> Anyone who practices these spiritual principles is bound to experience success. In fact, the study and application of spiritual principles comes with success *guaranteed*.
>
> (ibid:20)

In more academic discussions of leadership, religious concepts and ideas also abound. Discussion of the importance of leadership 'vision' (a Middle English word by origin, meaning a supernatural apparition) and 'mission' (mid-sixteenth-century origins, meaning to send the Holy Spirit into the world) routinely surface. So too does the concept 'charisma' which, despite the largely discredited nature of individualising trait-based understandings of leadership (Jackson and Parry 2011), is central to several theories, not least transformational leadership (Bass 1985; Bass and Avolio 1993). Originating in the Hellenistic word *kharisma*, meaning divine favour or supernatural power, the term was adopted by Christians of the New Testament period to refer to gifts such as prophecy that were understood as given by God to the faithful (for example, 1 Corinthians 12, 4–11). Weber (1947:358–359) subsequently drew the word into his ideal types of authority to refer to those 'endowed with . . . exceptional powers and qualities not accessible to the ordinary person but are regarded as of divine origin or as exemplary, and on the basis of them the individual concerned is treated as a leader' (Weber 1947:358–359, cited in Conger 2011:86). Such divine and exceptional qualities seem to have become rather assumed characteristics of modern leadership, with most business leaders being ascribed charismatic qualities today—or offered helpful advice on how to learn to be charismatic (for example, Antonakis, Fenley and Liechti 2012).

Business leadership is accorded further divine legitimation in the academic theories of *Spiritual Leadership* and *Servant Leadership*. Between them, Spiritual Leadership and Servant Leadership clock up over 800,000 hits on Google scholar at the time of my writing this sentence; there are dedicated academic journals (*The Journal of Spirituality, Leadership and Management* and *The Journal of Management, Spirituality and Religion*) and special issues of general leadership journals (e.g. *The Leadership Quarterly* 2005); and the American Academy of Management has had a Management, Spirituality and Religion Special Interest Group since 2001. The construction of Spiritual Leadership within the academic leadership field can be traced to the mid-1990s, with Fairholm's (1996) 'Spiritual Leadership: Fulfilling Whole-Self Needs at Work' credited as amongst the first (Dent et al. 2005, cited in Fernando 2011). Fairholm (1996:11) argues that 'non intuitive, leaner, rational management' and the 'abandonment of the traditional psychological contract connecting workers to a life-long career with the company' have 'destroyed the security and tranquillity of the workplace'. We are told that a growing number of people are seeking to solve this problem by connecting work and spirit. Enter business leaders who, as spiritual leaders, 'clarify followers' moral identities and strengthen and deepen their commitments. Spiritual leaders make connections between others' interior worlds of moral reflection and the outer worlds of work and social relationships' (ibid:12–13). The leader does so by managing not through the 'values of self-interest', but rather according to 'transcendent values' that draw heavily upon 'Judeo-Christian teachings', that are also 'core American values' (ibid:12).

Building upon Fairholm's beginnings, Fry and colleagues have developed what is probably the 'most extensively tested and validated' Spiritual

Leadership theory (Fernando 2011), though it perhaps should be noted that much of this testing and validation is at Fry and his colleagues' own hands. Fry's work initially promises a denominationally inclusive, even post-religious, approach to the spiritual (e.g. 2003:706, 2005:859). Though this is undercut somewhat by his adopting of a continuum that sees atheism described as 'founded upon despair and hopelessness' (2003:706) as one extreme and polytheistic religions 'with their bewildering multitude of defied natural gods' (p. 707) as the other. In the privileged centre sits ethical monotheism ('which Christianity shares with Judaism and Islam' p. 707) and we are told that, in any event, 'upon the scrutiny of philosophic inquiry' (p. 707) humanistic and pantheistic conceptions tend to converge around this Christian-and-other mean anyway. Fry defines the purpose of Spiritual Leadership to be to 'create vision and value congruence across the strategic, empowered team, and individual levels and, ultimately, to foster higher levels of organizational commitment and productivity' (ibid:693). The business leader as spiritual leader creates an 'intrinsic motivation cycle based on vision (performance), altruistic love (reward) and hope/faith (effort)'; this 'results in an increase in ones sense of spiritual survival (e.g. calling and membership) and ultimately positive organizational outcomes' such as 'increased commitment, productivity and continuous improvement' (Fry, Vitucci and Cedillo 2005:839). Each of the elements of this top-down 'intrinsic' motivation cycle is broken down into further qualities. For instance, the altruistic love-based reward system focuses upon employee demonstrations of trust/loyalty, forgiveness/acceptance/gratitude, integrity, honesty, courage, humility, kindness, compassion and patience/meekness/endurance. Notwithstanding this choice of humble terms, Fry's work lends itself to a particularly muscular form of spirituality. For example, the spiritual is subordinate to the performative: thus 'to be of benefit to leaders and their organizations, any definition of workplace spirituality must demonstrate its utility by impacting performance, turnover, and productivity and other relevant effectiveness criteria' (Fry 2003:703). Thankfully, however, and '(m)ost importantly from a management, leadership, and organizational perspective . . . is the finding by Mitroff and Denton (1999) that spirituality could be the ultimate competitive advantage' (ibid:703). Further, the way that 'spiritual' values are conceptualised in Fry's research might also give us some pause. For example, Fry and colleagues' early empirical work examined the Spiritual Leadership at the Apache Longbow helicopter attack squadron at Fort Hood, Texas. That we might struggle to square the nature of the work of these 'professional warrior soldiers' (Fry, Vitucci and Cedillo 2005:840) of this helicopter attack squadron with a study of the spiritual values of 'altruistic love', 'kindness', 'compassion', 'meekness' and 'forgiveness' seems not to have occurred to the authors. Indeed, we are told that 'the military is closer than most businesses in achieving the positive results of the Spiritual Leadership model', for already 'the army has adopted the majority of the Spiritual Leadership model components but under different terms' (ibid:854).

If Spiritual Leadership can be seen to reproduce a muscular, top-down and performance driven Judeo-Christian legitimation of business leadership, then Servant Leadership seems on the surface to promise something more conciliatory. Servant Leadership, which purports to cast the leader as servant to the organisation, its mission, and his/her followers, is typically understood to have originated in Robert Greenleaf's (1970) essay 'The Servant as Leader'. Greenleaf cites Herman Hesse's *Journey to the East* as inspiration for the work, though the text references an eclectic mix of further sources including the English theologian Dean Inge, Albert Camus, anarchist philosopher Paul Goodman, Alfred North Whitehead, St Francis, American physicist Percy Bridgman, Robert Frost, William Blake, Machiavelli, American Quaker John Woolman, Thomas Jefferson, Danish theologian Nikolai Frederik Severin Grundtvig, Paulo Freire, John Milton, Jesus, the precepts of Alcoholic Anonymous, Quakerism and Chilean philosopher of Esoteric Hitlerism Miguel Serrano. Despite these diverse sources, the 'theological roots of Greenleaf's essay', as Moreton (2010:110) observes, are 'obvious to the biblically literate'. References in the Bible to Jesus and/or the Messiah as servant, to his disciples as servants, and to the faithful and others as servants of God abound (for instance, Deuteronomy 9:27; Exodus 14:31; 32:13; Ezekiel 34:23–24; 37:24–25; Genesis 18:3; 32:10; Haggai 2:23; Isaiah 42:1–4; 49:1–7; 50:4–9; 52:13; Job 1:8; 42:7–8; Jude 1; Luke 22:27; Mark 10:45; Mathew 12:17–21; 20:28; Numbers 14:24; Psalm 105:6; Revelation 1:1; Romans 1:1). The relationship between religious discourse and Servant Leadership is more nuanced than a one-way borrowing of Christian service to re-legitimise business leadership however. For instance, the Episcopal Bishop of Atlanta, 'having encountered Greenleaf's writings soon after his appointment to the See in 1971 . . . was so inspired by the notion that he dedicated himself to "putting theology at the service of business" via an executive training institute at Emory University' (Moreton 2010:110). And Kenneth Blanchard, author of the best-selling (1982) *One-Minute Manager*, becomes a strong advocate for Servant Leadership following his own Christian conversion. He was to write the books *Servant Leader* (2003), *Lead Like Jesus* (2008) (both with Phil Hodges), and *Lead Like Jesus Revisited* (2016) (with Phil Hodges and Phyllis Hendry), and start the organisations *FaithWalk Leadership Institute* and *Lead Like Jesus*, both promoting an explicitly Christian Servant Leadership. For example, at *LeadLikeJesus.com* we are informed that:

> From Ugandan tribal kings to Ukrainian Christians, leaders around the world come face to face with Jesus through the global arm of Lead Like Jesus. . . . From pastors to mid-level managers, leaders are starting their journeys toward leading like Jesus. Lead Like Jesus

workshops will help you understand how God created you, how Jesus leads, and how you can become a leader more like Jesus.

Indeed, the concepts of Servant Leadership and Spiritual Leadership are so intertwined with the religious that an internet search of the term is as likely today to return pages on Church leadership and the leadership of Christian communities as it will return discussions of business leadership. Given such intersections, considering the use of a concept like Servant Leadership in these wider Christian communities may also give us further insight into the appeal of these ideas in the business realm. Moreton (2010) observes that in conservative Christian circles in the US, the mid-1970s saw a rapid growth of home-based churches. Building upon conservative Christian opposition to progressive movements of the 1960s, these home-based churches promoted an 'extreme form of patriarchal authority', according to which an older male 'shepherd' as the 'servant leader' exercised strict control over the life decisions of his flock (ibid:111). Such practices would morph into more established congregational doctrines over the following decade, such that in 1998 the largest Protestant denomination in the US 'explicitly couched its controversial message about female submission in terms of husband's "servanthood"' (ibid:112). And while figures such as Bill McCartney, founder of the all-male Christian organisation *Promise Keepers*, might claim that 'We're not talking about lording authority. We're talking about servanthood. There's a big difference' (in Moreton 2010:113), servanthood and Servant Leadership provided a religious legitimation for existing hierarchies, a buffer against calls for equality and codified an attitude of submission. This was not, however, to be submission by the leader—notwithstanding the language of service now used to describe their work. Rather Servant Leadership, in the conservative Christian household, in the Church, and in business too, required the submission of the 'led'.

## Hubris or the Man Who Would Be God

Given the unprecedented income inequalities, the deregulation and corporate consolidations, and the range of divine and other discourses legitimising their sacralised sovereignty, it might come as no surprise that hubris could surface in some quarters of business leadership—and it is this concept that I would like to end the chapter with. Hubris has received psychological, behavioural and psychiatric readings in leadership literatures (Sadler-Smith et al. 2017). However, its etymological roots—Ancient Greek for a presumptuous attitude towards the gods—suggest something than tallies more with the sacralised nature of leadership and those 'fantasies of omniscience and omnipotence [that] come to be enacted at the highest levels of organization' (Roberts 2001:119). For example, hubris, in the form of joining their corporate practices with a Christian religiosity, dripped from the ways that executives at the once eulogised, then criminally fraudulent, company *Enron* spoke of their work.

> If you walk around the halls here, people have a mission. The mission is we're on the side of angels. . . . We're bringing the benefits of choice and free markets to the world.
>
> (Jeffrey Skilling, then CEO of Enron, *Business Week* Online Extra, 2001)

> There was one meeting in particular that everyone at Enron remembers as marking the moment Kinder became the boss. In Enron mythology, it came to be known as the Come to Jesus meeting.
>
> (McLean and Elkind 2003:25)

> 'We saw things no one else could see.' Amanda Martin, another former executive, added, 'In the beginning, it was brilliant, we were riding a train, we were proselytizing. We were the apostles. We were right'.
>
> (ibid:38)

> Skilling loved to say that in trying to create a new kind of energy company, Enron was doing 'the Lord's work.' Mark struck a similar tone in talking about her business. 'We are brought together with a certain amount of missionary zeal,' she told Harvard for a case study. 'We are bringing the market mentality and spreading the privatization gospel in countries that desperately need this kind of thinking'.
>
> (ibid:71, quoting Enron CEO Jeff Skilling and CEO of Enron International, Rebecca Mark)

> Skilling's handful of direct reports, noted Alkhayat, the COO's Egyptian-born aide, operated with his 'blessed hand'; it was as if they'd been anointed by the leader as infallible and holy.
>
> (ibid:124)

Even when in a state of dis*grace*, executives evoked God to this cause. CEO Kenneth Lay sought spiritual support from ministers, telling one that he believed he could save Enron and wanted to do it 'God's way' (McLean and Elkind 2003:385). He received solace from his son Mark, enrolled at Southwestern Baptist Theological Seminary, who emailed reminding him of the tale of King Hezekiah, a ruler under siege, whom God saved by sending the angel of Jehovah to smite the Assyrians (ibid:385–386).

Outside of Enron's fall, hubris may be seen in the actions of numerous other business leaders, executives and corporations—indeed, it might be found in every corporate mission statement proclaiming the desire to be 'the world's leading. . . .' Perhaps, however, it is most notable today when business leaders venture into the area that the Christian and Judaic God explicitly removed from humankind. In *Genesis*, Adam and Eve are cast out of Eden for eating of the tree of knowledge. This banishment imposes the sentence of mortality. By being sent away humankind can no longer 'take also of the tree of life, and eat, and live for ever' (3:22). Immortality, however, is a new frontier of hubris for business leaders.

Quests for symbolic immorality may be seen in Elon Musk's *SpaceX* mission to seed a new Eden on Mars; the establishment of self-named charitable foundations such as *The Gates Foundation* or *The Chan Zuckerberg Initiative* and edifices like *Trump Tower* or Apple's new headquarters, 2.8 million square feet of meticulously planned legacy by a dying Steve Jobs. Inheritance too marks a kind of immortality, at least when one's children are inheriting the kinds of wealth that sacralised supermanagers are able to pass down.

In addition to symbolic attempts at immortality, we have funding by business leaders of some of the world's biggest tech companies of institutes and organisations seeking to unlock actual immortality. *The Lawrence Ellison Foundation*, for instance (started by the co-founder and ex-CEO of Oracle, with a portion of his estimated $60 billion new worth: Forbes.com), 'supports basic biomedical research on aging relevant to understanding lifespan development processes and age-related diseases and disabilities' (www.ellisonfoundation.org). The Google/Apple offshoot company *Calico* (an acronym for *California Life Company*) was started with a billion dollars of funding in 2013 (Friend 2017) and focuses upon 'health and well-being, in particular the challenge of aging and associated diseases' (Google Announcement 2013). Such projects have been likened to

> the Medici building a Renaissance chapel in Italy, but with a little extra Silicon Valley narcissism thrown in. It's based on the frustration of many successful rich people that life is too short: 'We have all this money, but we only get to live a normal life span'.
>
> (a scientist, familiar with *Calico*, quoted in Friend 2017)

Yuval Noah Harari examines similar developments in his (2016) *Homo Deus: A Brief History of Tomorrow*, arguing that

> the most interesting place in the world from a religious perspective is not the Islamic State or the Bible Belt, but Silicon Valley. That's where hi-tech gurus are brewing for us brave new religions that have little to do with God, and everything to do with technology. They promise all the old prizes—happiness, peace, prosperity and even eternal life—but here on earth with the help of technology, rather than after death with the help of celestial beings.
>
> (ibid:462)

As hubristic actions by sacralised business leaders go, the search for immortality surely ranks highest. There are numerous critiques that we might make of an aspiration for immortality. The old prophet of the market, Adam Smith, for example had something interesting to say about this topic. In *The Theory of Moral Sentiments*, Smith understood death to be 'one of the most important principles of human nature'. Not least because a mortal limit on the lifespan of any human served as bastion against tyranny. All humans, no matter how rich or powerful in their lifetime and no matter how they may wish to be gods, died. Mortality, ultimately, was the last 'great restraint upon the injustice of mankind, which, while it afflicts and mortifies the individual, guards and protects the society' (1759[2013]:5). However, as Eagleton (2010:151) has observed,

> many of the rich and powerful come to believe after a while that they are immortal and invincible. . . . As a result of this belief, such individuals come to wield the destructive power of gods. Only those whose circumstances make them conscious of their mortality are likely to feel solidarity with others of their kind.

If super-rich sacralised business leaders manage to achieve perpetual life, perhaps we all are damned. Though if we are, it seems we will not be alone—as the following chapter's examination of the long-historical association of the figure of the Devil, and the concept of evil, to capitalist business relations shows.

# 3  Devils

> . . . the damned are too proud to submit to limit. They will not bow the
> knee to the finite, least of all to their own creatureliness.
> Terry Eagleton (2010:26) *On Evil* (© Terry Eagleton. Reproduced
> with permission of the Licensor through PLSclear)

The Devil is the longest-standing, most consistently used figure deployed
to voice a critique of capitalist accumulation and organisation (Lizardo
2009): predating, for instance, Karl Marx's penchant for gothic figures
such as vampires, spectres, werewolves, gravediggers and zombies by
several hundred years. A proliferation of accounts and accusations of
individuals selling their soul and signing blood pacts for unholy personal
gain shows the Devil to have already been inextricably bound up in the
West with the business contract by the early modern period. Notable
examples include Christopher Marlowe's linking of usurious business
transactions, mercantile accumulation, and asymmetrical or extortionate
business contracts with the Devil in his retelling of the Faust legend; John
Milton's *Paradise Lost* which depicts Satan for the first time with a complex internal subjectivity, as a 'recognizably *capitalist* subject' (Lizardo
2009:608), even as 'the father of capitalism, bringing it into the world via
the temptation and the Fall' (Hand 2005:5 in Lizardo 2009:608); Johann
Wolfgang von Goethe's emplacing of Faust into a more recognisably early
industrial capitalist era, and in the process producing a representation
which is perhaps 'the most important representation of the "spirit" (in
the Weberian sense) of mature industrial capitalism, where the merchant's
interest in turning a profit is melded with the techno-rational subjugation
of natural forces' (Lizardo 2009:608); William Blake's *And did those feet
in ancient time* which first appeared in the preface to Blake's epic *Milton
a Poem*, and is best known today for the phrase 'dark satanic mills',
thought to refer to the large industrialised Albion flour mills located near
Blake's home; and, earlier even than each of these examples, Dante's
haunting stratified Hell of *L'Inferno* reproduced the 'complex labour
and boiling black pitch used in the Venice Arsenal, the largest form of

industrial organization that a 14th Century Florentine would have been aware' (Parker 2009:1292). Taking these and other literary and cultural evocations together,

> the Devil appears to have coevolved along with the development and rise to universal hegemony of certain Western institutions—in particular, the capitalist market and the bureaucratic state. Mirroring this development, the figure of the Devil becomes more 'rationalized' and less bestial and otherworldly, ultimately becoming internalized as a disembodied 'voice' within the individual subject.
>
> (Lizardo 2009:609)

Coming to the present day, the Devil is still widely evoked as a means of criticising nefarious business and organisational practice and 'continues to be one of the most pervasive symbols of the workings of capitalism and its historical penetration into communal and everyday life' (Lizardo 2009:605). In popular culture, the 'demonology of big organisations' (Parker 2002:134) is a recurrent theme in the products of the culture industries, and in Hollywood film the Devil 'continues to be an intuitive symbolic resource to "map" the global, consumer-based capitalist system in late modernity' (Lizardo 2009:605). Popular writing on CEOs and corporate malfeasance also evoke the Devil, demonic creatures and their realm. In an insider account of the fall of Lehman Brothers, for example, McDonald and Robinson (2009) recounted that 'there was something of the night' (McDonald and Robinson 2009:91) about the seldom seen CEO. 'I sensed there was something deeply disquieting about this oddball demigod who ruled everyone's lives. Quite simply, people were afraid of him, even though they couldn't see him' (McDonald and Robinson 2009:90); Bookstaber's (2007:6) critique of the US financial markets reflected that '(i)t would seem there is a demon unleashed, haunting the market and casting our efforts awry: a demon of our own design'; McLean and Nocera's (2010) analysis of the financial crisis was entitled *All the Devils Are Here*; and in the fanciful museum of corporate malfeasance that opens Flanagan's (2003) *Dirty Rotten CEOs*, sinning executives are consigned to the Devil and suffer for all eternity in ways demanded by Pope George the Great: boiling in oil for their greed, broken on a wheel for pride or standing in frozen water for envy. Academics are not immune to the Devil's lure either. For example, Ford and Harding (2003) utilised Marlowe's play *Dr Faustus* as an extended analogy to consider the lived experiences of organisational subjects in times of mergers, Koehn (2000, 2007) read managerial practices through analogy to Dante's *Inferno*, and Wray-Bliss (2012) and Ailon (2013) have examined the demonisation of fallen CEOs.

To illustrate the accessibility of the figure of the Devil as a means to represent nefarious CEO activity, we can compare Milton's (1667[2000]) seminal literary depiction of Satan in *Paradise Lost* with how disgraced CEO Jeff Skilling is represented in McLean and Elkind's (2003) examination of the collapse of Enron. Loewenstein (2004), in his introduction to the Cambridge University Press edition of *Paradise Lost*, draws out Milton's characterisation of Satan well. Milton's Satan is courageous and charismatic. He is an attractive yet perverse and wrathful character. A remarkably skilled rhetorician, he is capable of marshalling his troops in the face of the greatest adversary. He is uniquely ambitious. He is rationalistic, asserting the power of his mind alone to transform his environment. He is unrepentant and wilful, egotistical and arrogant: insistent that he is the creator of his own identity. And he is ultimately tragic, brought down by his own pride. Compare the above with representations in McLean and Elkind (2003) *The Smartest Guys in the Room*. With phrasing that evokes a luciferous nature, Skilling was 'the brooding, mercurial genius . . . the architect of Enron's greatest triumphs—and its ultimate disgrace' (ibid). He was 'incandescently brilliant' and could 'process information and conceptualize new ideas with blazing speed' (p. 28). 'Wherever Jeff was, talent would flock. The activity was following the light' (former Enron Vice President, Bob Schorr, quoted in McLean and Elkind 2003:120). From an unhappy childhood as, according to one friend, a 'tortured soul' (p. 29), Skilling presented as a wholly self-made man, thus we have the oft-repeated parable of his job, at age 13, of chief production director at the start-up Aurora (Illinois) television station (Zellner 2001). Skilling has been cast as one who believed that his brilliant intellect could fashion new worlds. Of his tenure at McKinsey, McLean and Elkind (2003:32) wrote, 'It would be hard to imagine a place that suited Skilling more perfectly. The McKinsey thought process reduced a chaotic world to a series of coolly clinical, logical observations. That's precisely how Skilling thought'. He carried this privileging of mind, idea and intellect into Enron, recruiting top-performing MBA graduates and mathematics PhDs over those with experience of the energy industry. Skilling refashioned the energy business with mark-to-market accounting practices and the skilful use of 'gaming' to out-think regulators. Skilling was hugely arrogant (pp. 32, 241, 245, 345): 'We could be the market maker for the world!' (Skilling in McLean and Elkind 2003:226). He was also wrathful if crossed, taking vengeful glee in undermining the contributions of the CEO of Enron International, Rebecca Mark, with whom he used to be in a relationship (pp. 110, 246, 255, 259). Despite his flaws of character and the eventual despised, and tragic, figure he was to become, Skilling's undoubted brilliance, arrogance, drive and intimidating intellect carried many along with him. Skilling was a remarkably skilled rhetorician,

> the Enron story, when Skilling told it, sounded so good; otherwise intelligent people were reduced to nodding heads in agreement . . . he

was a master presenter. He knew how to convey the sense of limitless opportunities and supercharged growth that investors wanted to hear.

(p. 233)

Tom Peters, who worked with Skilling at McKinsey in the early days, summed up Skilling's rhetorical brilliance with apposite phrasing: 'Skilling could out argue God' (Flanagan 2003:72).

## The Devil as Sovereign Subject

As the above historical and contemporary representations attest, the Devil—and the concept of evil that this figure is thought to embody—is a 'metaphysical notion that has infiltrated common sense' (Cole 2006:21). In the context of an American society, strongly influenced by a conservative Christianity, this common sense tends toward a binary, dualistic conceptualisation of good and evil (Singer 2004). For cultural historian Gerald Messadié, such a conceptualisation has both a long history and political effects. In *Historie Générale du Diable* (1996), Messadié presents a compelling phenomenological history of the Evil One—documenting his absence in Greek, Roman, Egyptian, Hindu and Chinese traditions, his birth in Zoroastrian Persia, adolescence in early Israel and maturity in the latter Islamic, Judaic and Christian faiths. Throughout the book, Messadié considers the social and political impact of the concept of evil in specific times and localities, as well as the connections between a society's religious views, its political views and its dominant institutions. On the whole, Messadié is relatively sanguine about humanity's conceptualisation of evil in much of our history. In the early societies of Oceania, China and Japan; in Mesopotamia; among the Celts; in Ancient Rome, Egypt and Africa; in South America; and among the North American native populations, Messadié meticulously charts the existence of numerous demons, demigods, mythic heroes, spirits and such. In these pantheistic and polytheistic cultures Messadié sees a form of religiosity that enables certain freedoms from priestly or other religiously sanctified hierarchical rule. Overpopulated pantheons, he argues, 'make for insubordinate mortals who are cynical about the immortals' and '(t)he clergy in polytheisms also seem to be less cohesive: what right does a priest of Apollo have to tell a priest of Aphrodite or Hermes how to go about his business?' (Messadié 1996:90).

Messadié's critique of the devil/evil, as opposed to his more descriptive historical excavations, is principally reserved for the social and political consequences that coincide with the ways evil and goodness are constructed in monotheistic religion. The birth and spread of monotheistic religion, with the figures of a personified and unique Devil waging war against a personified and unique God, is identified as originating some four millennia ago among the Kurgan horsemen occupying the Dnieper and Donetz basins, the low valley of the Volga and the Kazakhstan steppes—south of present-day Russia (Messadié 1996:72). The Kurgan people, whom we have since come to call Indo-Europeans, descended upon and settled in the more fertile plains of Iran, from where they spread their number, civilisation and beliefs to the Near and Middle East and Europe. Key to transforming and solidifying monotheistic religion in the region was the figure of Zoroaster (Zarathustra in ancient Persian)— probably born around 628 BC. Zoroastrian reforms led to the rejection of animal sacrifice and orgiastic rituals among the Iranian populous, and the eventual 'complete ban on the ancient gods and the rites associated with them, as well as a radical reorganization of the divine hierarchy . . . the unprecedented creation of a God–Devil pairing and of the equally unprecedented Good/Evil ethical dualism' (Messadié 1996:85). The dualistic personifications of evil in the figure of the Devil and good in the figure of a singular God, argues Messadié, engenders deeply problematic effects. Not least, a dualistic understanding of God/Devil lends itself to a politics of Othering: us/them, worthy/not worthy, mine/not mine and, ultimately, I and those that are not I.

In the long history of both theological and philosophical conceptualisations of the devil, such denial of others, this I/not I, was itself considered the root of evil. Within theology, influential early Christian scholar Augustine, for example, drew upon *Ecclesiasticus 10:13* ('For pride is the beginning of sin, and he that hath it shall pour out abomination: and therefore the Lord brought upon them strange calamities, and overthrew them utterly') to regard pride as the origin of all sin. Pride for Augustine, understood as belief in one's own sovereignty and lack of recognition of one's dependence upon and obligation owed to others—especially God—showed that 'man has become like the Devil . . . by living by the rule of self' (Augustine 427[1972]:552) and by regarding himself 'as his own light' (ibid:573). For Augustine it is but a small and easily trodden step to go from this sovereign self-regard to seek to dominate others for our own ends. Such an understanding is common across other Christian writers. John Calvin, for instance, whose reforming Protestantism figures so centrally in Weber's account of the birth of Capitalism, was to regard the root of evil similarly. In his most important work, *Institutes of the Christian Religion*, he writes that 'no one lives in a worse or more evil manner than he who lives and strives for himself alone, and thinks about and seeks only his own advantage' (cited in Blanchard 2010:29).

We find a similar damning of the desire for absolute sovereignty in religiously inspired literature. Milton's Satan denies his dependence and reliance on God; willing himself to believe that he is 'self-begot, self-rais'd/By [his] own quick'ning power' (Milton 1667[2000] 5.860–5.861). Indeed Satan's very name, meaning adversary in the original Hebrew, is as Forsythe (1987:4) observes both 'paradoxical and tragic. It defines a being who can only be contingent: as the adversary, he must always be a function of another, not an independent entity. As Augustine and Milton show, it is precisely when Satan imagines himself independent that he is most deluded'. Eagleton's (2010) *On Evil* shows other influential literary works to have conceptualised evil in similar terms. For example, there 'is something peculiarly pointless and malevolent in Shakespeare's mind about things that bring themselves to birth, feed upon themselves or define themselves tautologically in their own terms' (ibid:86). With reference to more recent literary works, Eagleton discusses the preoccupation of William Golding with the question of evil. The adolescent evils in *Lord of the Flies* are well known, however it is Golding's novel *Pincher Martin* that for Eagleton best maps the contours of being damned by self-regard and a denial of the other. The main character in the book, sailor Christopher Martin, is lost at sea with no means of survival, yet he cannot accept his fate. Though his physical body sinks beneath the waves—has done so in fact, as we later find out, from the very start of the novel—he cannot let go and give himself up to God. Deluding himself that his own heroic act of will has staved off death, and that he is now residing on a rocky outcrop in the sea, Martin is reduced to a crab-like scurrying around what turns out to be the contours of his own dying mind. Self-obsessed in life, he remains so after his physical body dies, refusing to give up the self which was all he ever had. It is Martin's lack of love for others, and his excess of self-love, that condemns him.

Conceptualising the root of evil as the dream of absolute sovereignty—as a denial of reliance upon and responsibility to others—provides theological and philosophical lineage to contemporary critiques of corporate practices. The severing of responsibility to others can be seen, for example, in the tax avoidance strategies of large corporations—strategies that rob society of the resources it needs to reproduce an equitable and compassionate existence for the population. Apple, for instance, in 2014 paid just 0.005% tax on its non-US-based profits—equivalent to just $50 tax on every million dollars it made (Kottasova 2016); figures from the Australian Tax Office show that more than a third of all the large companies operating out of Australia paid zero tax in 2014–2015; this included Qantas Airways which paid no tax on a $15bln income, Origin Energy which paid no tax on a $12bln income, and ExxonMobil Australia which paid no tax on an $8bln income, plus another 676 large corporations which also paid no tax; more broadly, Oxfam's (2016) research report, 'The Hidden Billions', found that in 2014 alone corporations operating in developing countries shifted US$638 billion to tax havens, resulting in an estimated loss of US$172 billion tax revenue to the governments of those populations of the world who are in direst need for the services and support that such tax revenue could provide. The use of tax havens to hoard income and deny duty to others is part of a long history of mercantilism.

Pre-Roman Empire city-states, including Tyre, Carthage and Utica, encouraged trade by declaring themselves 'free cities,' where goods in transit could be stored without tax, and merchants would be protected from harm. These tax-free areas developed further economic significance during colonial times, when entire cities-including Hong Kong, Singapore and Gibraltar-were designated as 'free ports' from which the loot of colonialism could be safely shipped back to England, Europe or America with low import tariffs.

(Klein 2000:204)

In terms of severing of responsibilities, the free cities and free ports of old are outdone today by the free trade zone/export-processing zone.

Though it has plenty in common with these other tax havens, the export processing zone is really in a class of its own. Less holding tank than sovereign territory, the EPZ is an area where goods don't just pass through but are actually manufactured, an area, furthermore, where there are no import and export duties, and often no income or property taxes either.

(ibid)

Multinational capital's use of these zones to outsource and subcontract production, to so divest themselves of all responsibility for the persons who make their products, and the below-subsistence wages and appalling conditions of work in these zones are by now well documented. The corporate 'race to the bottom' in the search for ever cheaper global labour and ever more loosely regulated workplaces has human consequences. Over 1100 died at the Rana Plaza factory collapse, hundreds burned to death pressed against the locked doors and barred windows of their sweatshop workplaces, trade union organisers tortured and killed, suicides over working conditions, and despair at the erosion of dignity and the dying of hope that unreasonably hard work, producing the products stamped by a global brand, will ever generate more than the most meagre subsistence living. 'When the actual manufacturing process is so devalued, it stands to reason that the people doing the work of production are likely to be treated like detritus—the stuff left behind' (Klein 2000:197).

Corporate severing of responsibility for employees doesn't stop at the borders of free trade zones, of course. Downsizing, subcontracting, casualisation, work-intensification and zero-hour contracts blight the working landscape of both developing and developed nations. In the US, for example, it has been predicted that by 2020 around half of all US workers will be in what the government terms 'contingent employment'. In Japan, by 2015, just short of 40% were contingent and in South Korea 'non-regular' workers accounted for around 33% of the workforce (Herod and Lambert 2016). Nearly 40% of Australian employees have insecure work (The Guardian 2018). Such contingent or non-regular employment can be brutal. China's rapidly urbanising assent to modernity, for example, is being built with the labour of peasant workers from Hebei, Shandong, Hunan, Henan, Jiangsu and Sichuan provinces (Ngai and Huilin 2016). Employed as labour-only subcontractors in a newly 'modernised' (deregulated and privatised) building industry, these workers leave their provinces and families for year-long relocation to the city construction sites. Here they are not entitled to their pay until the end of either six months' (those from Hebei, Henan and Shandong province) or a year's labour (those from Sichuan, Hubei and Hunan). Until then they subsist on an irregular minimal living allowance. Come the end of 6 or 12 months of hard and dangerous construction work, many are either not paid at all or are paid a fraction of what was promised. Legal redress is minimal. Subcontracting firms either disband or are in thrall to other subcontracted parties. Or the year-long labour without pay is reclassified as a pre-modern form of willing 'labour service', excluded from the legal protections due to wage labourers (ibid:136–137).

Such precarious employment practices, along with corporate tax avoidance and global outsourcing, may each be defined by a denial of responsibilities to others, a desire to act as if the corporation were sovereign and autonomous. For figures as central and significant for Christianity as Augustine and Ecclesiastics, this desire for sovereignty was the very root of evil.

## Natural and Moral Evils

Despite the ground already traversed, we haven't fully mapped the terrain of evil yet. Even if we restrict ourselves to Christianity's sacred texts, we have further to go. The pairing of an absolute personified evil (the Devil) competing with an absolute personified good, for example, is itself contestable. While the New Testament *Book of Revelation* would personify evil in the 'great dragon . . . that ancient serpent, who is called the Devil and Satan, the deceiver of the world' (*Revelation/Apocalypse* 12:7b–9) and who stands as 'God's quintessential Other' (Beal 2002:78), a clear cosmic dualism of good versus evil, God versus Devil, 'is completely unprecedented in light of earlier biblical tradition' (ibid:80). In the Old Testament, for instance, the term satan is quite ambivalent. Frequently, it refers to several different characters that act as satans—as deceivers and tempters. At other times it does refer to a distinct being and one that occasions suffering. However, this Satan is one of God's heavenly court, and the harms it occasions are done entirely under God's instruction and consent. Rather than this Satan being a figure of absolute otherness, it is an obedient underling of God, albeit one that does the more unpalatable bidding of its master. Satan's commands still originate with God, and this underscores the light and dark, benevolent and destructive nature of the God of the Old Testament (Cole 2006). It is only with the transformation of an ambivalent Old Testament God into a wholly benign, loving God of the New Testament that evil must be explained as something that arises as an external force opposing the will of God.

The construction, however, of an external opposing evil raises significant problems for a belief system that is founded upon the idea of an omnipotent benevolent God. As Bayle in his influential Enlightenment text, *Dictionnaire Historique et Critique*, observed:

> God is either willing to remove evil and cannot; or he can and is unwilling; or he is neither willing nor able to do so; or else he is both willing and able. If he is willing and not able, he must then be weak, which cannot be affirmed of God. If he is able and not willing, he must be envious, which is also contrary to the nature of God. If he is neither willing nor able, he must be both envious and weak, and consequently not be God. If he is both willing and able—the only possibility that agrees with the nature of God—then where does evil come from?

> (Bayle 1697[1965]:169 in Neiman 2002:118)

Attempts to answer such a question and to square the answer away with belief in a just God (or in secular terms a good society) are called *theodicies*—after Liebniz's book of the same name. Writing on the cusp of modernity, Liebniz would seek to marry rationality with a belief in God, so as to 'prove the conformity of faith with reason' (Neiman 2002:21). For Liebniz, it was self-evident that what were regarded as natural evils— storms, floods, drought, volcanic eruptions and the like—were God's punishment for humankind's moral evils. Though we may not understand why we were being punished in such apparently indiscriminate ways, the punishment must be warranted as it arose from the actions of a loving and omnipotent creator. The catastrophic natural event of the 1755 earthquake, which wholly destroyed the prosperous and civilised city of Lisbon, however, would shake early Enlightenment thinking on this matter to the core. Figures as significant to the Enlightenment as Kant, Voltaire and Rousseau wrote and debated on the meaning of this disaster. A child-age Goethe was said to have been 'brought to doubt and consciousness for the first time' by the event (Neiman 2002:1). It seemed inconceivable that the inhabitants of this civilised and modern city could possibly have committed evils warranting such severe divine retribution. Seeking to account for this event laid one of the crucial pieces of later theodicies: the radical separation of natural from moral evil (ibid:4). Moral evils—the evils that humankind do—would be theological and, increasingly, philosophical matters. Natural evils would be progressively moved from the realms of theology and metaphysics, with their categories of ethics and evil, and emplaced in the realm of science. Thus, for example, Immanuel Kant— still then to become the Enlightenment's greatest moral philosopher and strongest proponent for emplacing ethics squarely in the realm of human intentionality—wrote three essays for the Königsberg newspaper following the Lisbon catastrophe, explaining the nature of earthquakes with the scientific explanations available at the time (ibid:1). Liebniz's theodicy, his causality between the moral evils of humankind and catastrophic natural evils, had suffered a seemingly fatal blow.

Seemingly fatal that is until our anthropogenic present brought the arguments underlying Liebniz's theodicy once again to the heart of the severest existential threat we face. It is now the Enlightenment's progeny—scientists—however that are compelled to draw a Liebnizian connection between human action and natural events: between industrial pollution, industrial waste, mass deforestation, for instance, and unprecedented $CO_2$ levels, planetary warming, the melting of arctic ice and permafrost, and the start of mass extinction events. It is conservative and corporate voices that are denying such connection, cleaving to what had hitherto been modernity's confident separation of natural from moral evils. And the use of this term *evil* to describe the actions of major corporations in this regard starts perhaps to seem less anachronistic the more we find out. For example, in their 2008 article in *Environmental Politics*, Jacques, Dunlap and Freeman examine the actions of corporately funded conservative think tanks in manufacturing a climate change 'debate'. Originating as organised conservative counter-movement to the advances made by progressive politics in the 1960s, then later employed by the tobacco and pesticide industries to attempt to confuse the scientific link between their products and cancer, conservative think tanks function by producing 'an endless flow of printed material ranging from books to editorials designed for public consumption to policy briefs aimed at policy-makers and journalists, combined with frequent appearances by spokespersons on TV and radio' (ibid:355). In the realm of climate change, these corporately funded think tanks have flooded the public domain with climate sceptic material in an attempt to 'manufacture doubt' and cast the scientific consensus as left-wing bias and junk science. For example, of the climate sceptic books published in the US between 1972 and 2005, Jacques, Dunlap and Freeman found that 92% of these were directly linked to conservative think tanks. In this area, and in their other areas of conservative and corporate advocacy, these think tanks 'have become exceptionally influential in US politics' (ibid:355). *The Climate Deception Dossiers* (2015), produced by the Union of Concerned Scientists, document similar corporate tactics of denying or muddying the link between human agency and climate change. Compiled from an analysis of internal fossil fuel industry memos and documents, the dossier reveals 'a coordinated campaign underwritten by the world's major fossil fuel companies and their allies to spread climate misinformation and block climate action' (ibid:1). These tactics include 'collusion', 'the use of front groups to hide companies' influence and avoid accountability', 'the secret funding of purportedly independent scientists', and sending members of Congress forged letters 'claiming to be from nonprofits that advocate for the wellbeing of women, minorities, children, seniors, and veterans' that aim to persuade against supporting climate legislation (ibid)—a tactic that brings to mind the Trump administration's Energy Chief Rick Perry's claim that fossil fuels prevent sexual assault (Roberts 2017). Other documents, including a bundle released to a US court in 2015, show the fossil fuel companies to have known of the causal link between the burning of fossil fuels, $CO_2$ emissions and dangerous climate change for decades. Scientists working for the anachronistically named Humble Oil (now ExxonMobil), for example, published research linking fossil fuels to rising $CO_2$ levels as early as 1957; a 1978 Exxon management briefing paper charted 'serious consequences' of 'human-caused emissions' leading to the 'Greenhouse Effect'; and Exxon's External Affairs Manager sent a primer on climate change to Exxon management in 1982, describing the 'potentially catastrophic events' that will occur if fossil fuel use is not reduced (Greenpeace n.d.). Yet Exxon continued to be a 'leader in campaigns of confusion' around climate change for the next 40 years (Hall 2015), denying causal links between fossil fuels and climate change and spending over US\$30 million funding climate denial think tanks since 1981 (Greenpeace n.d.).

Might we call such actions evil? In *The Atrocity Paradigm: A Theory of Evil* (2002), Claudia Card presents a philosophical redefinition of evil. For Card,

> evils are foreseeable intolerable harms produced by culpable wrongdoing. On my theory, the nature and severity of the harms, rather than the perpetrators' psychological states, distinguishes evils from ordinary wrongs . . . Evildoers, however, are not necessarily malicious. Oftener they are inexcusably reckless, callously indifferent, amazingly unscrupulous.
>
> (Card 2002:3–4)

Obscuring the scientific link between fossil fuels, $CO_2$ and climate change to keep profiting from a product that you know to be leading to catastrophic harms for Earth's inhabitants would seem to readily fit Card's definition of evil: foreseeable intolerable harms produced by culpable wrongdoing by those who are inexcusably reckless, callously indifferent or amazingly unscrupulous.

## Necessary Evils

I have argued that Leibniz's pre-modern theodicy, linking the evils of human behaviour with catastrophic natural events, has new and chilling relevance in our anthropogenic age. And this may not be the only historical theodicy that is relevant to the present.

Bernard de Mandeville's controversial Enlightenment text *The Fable of the Bees: or Private Vices, Publick Benefits* provided a secularised theodicy that linked individual vices to a wider public good. Organised around a poetic fable, and surrounding prose explanations, of an industrious and productive hive of bees all pursuing their own selfish ends, which is rendered unproductive and fallow once these bees become virtuous and honest, Mandeville's intent was to

> shew the Impossibility of enjoying all the most elegant Comforts of Life that are to be met with in an industrious, wealthy and powerful nation, and at the same time be bless'd with all the Virtue and Innocence that can be wish'd for in a Golden Age . . . those very Vices of every particular Person by skilful Management, were made subservient to the Grandeur and worldly Happiness of the whole.
>
> (Mandeville 1723:2)

In his lecture on Mandeville to the British Academy, architect of neoliberalism F. A. Hayek argued that Mandeville's *Fable of the Bees* provided the first of what he calls 'modern theories of society' (Hayek 1967:131). By this he seems to mean a view of society that accorded with his own; that is, a society which develops and functions absent of rational planning or deliberate government effort; one where 'that universal mover in human nature, SELF-LOVE' (Tucker 1755, in Hayek 1967:134) directs the efforts of each individual; and evolutionary processes translate these individual selfish desires into a productive whole. While his interpretation of Mandeville is contentious, particularly as to whether Mandeville's 'skilful Management' suggests a role for rational planning and not the *laissez-faire* situation that Hayek desires to reads it as, Hayek builds Mandeville into a grand edifice of evolutionary-based thought (in which he includes Adam Smith, David Hume, Charles Darwin and others), which he sees as legitimising the spontaneous, market-based ordering of society.

For Hayek, Mandeville's work is irreligious, presenting the first argument that morality in humankind is not implanted from without as an act of theistic design, but rather is an outcome of a process of evolution. Hayek characterises this rejection of design arguments as no less than the production of 'what we call the modern mind' (ibid:141). Despite Hayek's arguments, however, economics and theology are not so easily separated (Waterman 2002). Indeed, Richard T. Ely, the leading figure in the creation of the American Economic Association in 1885, for instance, advocated for the new profession of economics to be located in schools of theology (Nelson 1993). Hayek's desire to cast neoliberalism as an entirely secular evolutionary science is also quite questionable. This can perhaps best be seen by Hayek's attempt to emplace the works of Adam Smith into the evolution tradition (Hayek 1967).

Adam Smith continued Mandeville's earlier arguments regarding the social good arising as an outcome of self-interested individual actions and drew from Mandeville the key phrase 'the division of labour'; however, he was far less cavalier than Mandeville regarding vice and venality. As a staunch Victorian moralist, Presbyterian and advocate for the Calvinist Church of Scotland, Smith placed great store on self-restraint and self-command; 'to restrain our selfish, and to indulge our benevolent affections, constitutes the perfection of human nature' (Smith 1759:1.1.44). Smith was to regard human moral sympathy towards others as common to all persons, '(h)ow selfish soever man may be supposed, there are evidently some principles in his nature, which interest him in the fortunes of others, and render their happiness necessary to him' (Smith 1759:1.1.1). Notwithstanding this, Smith accepted that much human action, particularly in the economic realm, is directed towards a form of self-interest. Where Mandeville would have his 'skilful Management' to turn the private vices into public goods, Smith we know wrote of an *invisible hand* guiding human behaviour. There is debate regarding the centrality of this particular phase in Smith's work (Rothschild 1994), not least because it only occurs three times in all of Smith's writings. However, the idea of a providential force, shaping individual human actions towards the direction of a teleological generalised good, has been seen as essential to understanding Smith's *oeuvre*: 'for Smith the logic of spontaneous order rests on the "fact" that the world with all its miraculous equilibria is the product of a benign and loving creative demiurge' (Hill 2001:22). Rather than the irreligious proto-Darwinian evolutionist that Hayek wishes to cast him, Smith's economics is probably therefore better understood in the tradition of the natural theology of Newton's *Principia* (Waterman 2002; Milbank 1990): an attempt to use science and rationality to understand the intricate mechanisms through which God has organised the laws of the natural world, or, for Smith, the laws of the world of economic production and exchange.

In addition to Hayek's questionable recruitment of Smith to the evolutionary cause, it is fair to say that Smith's invisible hand has been appropriated to eulogise for and excuse levels of selfishness and disregard of others which would have been quite abhorrent for the Scottish moralist Smith.

> No society can surely be flourishing and happy, of which the far greater part of the members are poor and miserable. It is but equity, besides, that they who feed, clothe, and lodge the whole body of the people, should have such a share of the produce of their own labour as to be themselves tolerably well fed, clothed, and lodged.
>
> (Smith 1776, Book 1, Ch 8, paragraph 36, *Wealth of Nations*)

As a key figure co-opted into neoliberalism, Smith's prevailing upon employers to provide wages suitable for at least a tolerable life might be seen to represent something of an embarrassment for twenty-first-century corporations running their 'race to the bottom' in search for ever cheaper and more disposable labour. All is not lost, however, for those desiring a neoliberal theodicy. Unlikely as it might seem, succour can be found again in religion. Observing that the Reagan administration marked the first election to figure the evangelical Christian Right as a powerful and mobilised political bloc constituency, Kaplan (2004:72) argues that the

> conservative economic agenda of lower taxes, deregulation, and downsizing government seemed perfectly tailored to fundamentalist Christians . . . the evangelical movement emphasized personal responsibility, through the life-changing experience of being born again.

Neoliberal inequality too can be reconciled within a religious tradition. In his discussion of the roots of the spirit of capitalism, Weber (1930[2001]) observed that Calvinism represented a much harsher, more extremely inhuman (ibid:60) doctrine than did Catholicism. Under Calvinism, one must not presume that one's actions could affect God's eternal decrees and absolute free will in any way. 'For the damned to complain of their lot would be much the same as for animals to bemoan the fact that they were not born as men' (ibid:60). Translated into a modern spirit of capitalism, this may help explain a sense of entitlement amongst senior executives and a seeming lack of fellow-feeling towards the outsourced, redundant or precariously employed: despite the rhetorical appeal to being 'self-made-men [sic]', stations of success (or otherwise) are prior providential givens. Even the shining centrepiece of neoliberal subjectivity, the accumulation of personal wealth, finds religious support. Calvinist Protestantism, as Blanchard (2010) observes, was never a religion of asceticism. Becoming wealthy and enjoying the pleasures that such wealth brings was natural and good, providing that such enjoyment was somewhat temperate. And Protestants were never enjoined to leave their fortunes to the Church, given Martin Luther's original protest against the purchase of remission from sin. Translating Calvin's natural enjoyment of wealth into a rather less-temperate modern-day US, Evangelical and Charismatic Protestant preachers proclaim a controversial but highly popular 'prosperity gospel', the central message of which is 'that God directly dispenses divine favours in the capitalist marketplace to his steadfast believers' (Lehman 2016). The prosperity gospel, writes Bowler (2015:631), may be understood as

> the Protestant work ethic . . . folded into an entirely mental world. . . . This was the arduous work of the prosperity gospel, those small acts of cultivating an alternative imagination and learning how to recast spiritual lives as labour measureable in divine currency and redeemable for earthly rewards.
>
> (Bowler 2015:631)

As Sullivan and Delaney (2016:841) observe, the prosperity gospel

> is decidedly neoliberal in that it blends a belief in the 'power of the individual with the idea that capitalist society provides equal opportunity for all' (Machado 2010:729). It therefore affirms popular images of the enterprising individual that characterize American mythology, where it is argued the 'free market rewards every entrepreneur without limit' (Cahn 2008:430). The subject produced within this discourse are a 'new kind of neoliberal twenty-first-century Christian' who 'understands that material consumption is a good thing, even a godly act' (Machado 2010:729).

Combining, amongst other sources, the self-proclaimed secularism of Hayek, the cynicism of Mandeville, the natural theology of Smith and the expectant avarice of the modern prosperity gospel, neoliberal theodicy reconciles what might otherwise be regarded as individual evils with the idea of a greater good. Private vice, self-love, monetary greed and rampant consumption are transubstantiated through the providential hand of a magical unseen force, 'the market', into the good and free society.

## Radical and Banal Evil

If, however, we do not choose to ascribe to a neoliberal theodicy and excuse individual evils in the economic realm as a necessary component of a greater neoliberal good, then perhaps we need to seek to understand why evils occur. In seeking to do this, despite its long-standing use to represent evils of capitalism, the figure of the Devil may not help us much. Moral philosophers have long contested the idea that human beings are capable of acts of devilish evil—that is, of willing evil for its own end. Thomas Hobbes, for example, though most pessimistic regarding human morality generally, wrote in *Leviathan*, 'that any man should take pleasure in other mens great harmes, without other end of his own, I do not conceive it possible' (Hobbes 1651[1985:126] in Cole 2006:17). 'Absolute, unprovoked, disinterested malice', David Hume argued a century later in *An Enquiry Concerning the Principles of Morals* (1751[1975]:227 in ibid), 'has never perhaps place in any human breast'. And the greatest of the Enlightenment moralists, Immanuel Kant, though clear-eyed regarding the myriad ways the call of morality is eluded, considered it impossible for human beings to will evil maxims. For each of these figures, being human entailed being subject to the call of morality (Cole 2006), and though we may twist this morality and we may ignore it or trade it off against other motives, it nevertheless still echoes in our conscience.

Carrying these arguments into the modern era, Hannah Arendt, more than any other writer of the twentieth century, has been responsible for presenting us a conceptualisation of evil that resists demonising the evil doer—even when the acts that individuals commissioned and committed were atrocities. 'It is indeed my opinion', wrote Arendt, 'that evil is never "radical", that it is only extreme, and that it possesses neither depth nor any demonic dimension. It can overgrow and lay waste the whole world precisely because it spreads like a fungus on the surface' (Arendt 1964a:56). Reporting on the trial for war crimes of senior Nazi Otto Adolf Eichmann, Arendt wrote not of the radicality but rather the 'banality' of Eichmann's evil:

> Half a dozen psychiatrists had certified him as 'normal'—'More normal, at any rate, than I am after having examined him,' one of them was said to have exclaimed. . . . Behind the comedy of the soul experts lay the hard fact that his was obviously no case of moral let alone legal insanity . . . his was obviously also no case of insane hatred of Jews; on the contrary, he had plenty of 'private reasons' for not being a Jew-hater . . . Alas, nobody believed him. The prosecutor did not believe him . . . Counsel for the defense paid no attention. . . . And the judges did not believe him . . . too conscious of the very foundations of their profession, to admit that an average, 'normal' person, neither feeble-minded nor indoctrinated nor cynical, could be perfectly incapable of telling right from wrong . . . [as such they each] missed the greatest moral and even legal challenge of the whole case.
>
> (1963[2006]:25–26)

That Eichmann's evil was banal was never intended by Arendt to be a 'theory or doctrine' of evil, though, rather merely a statement of 'something quite factual' (1971a:159), 'which stared one in the face at the trial' (1963[2006]:287). Her theorising of evil and its causes focussed not upon what she had seen of evil's banality, but rather on the relationship of *thinking* to evil. As Arendt was to write later of Eichmann, 'the only specific characteristic one could detect in his past as well as in his behaviour during the trial and the preceding police examination was something entirely negative . . . . a curious, quite authentic inability to think' (1971a:159). Could, she asked,

> the activity of thinking as such, the habit of examining and reflecting upon whatever happens to come to pass, regardless of specific content and quite independent of results, could this activity be of such a nature that it 'conditions' men against evildoing?
>
> (Arendt 1971a:160)

For Arendt the answer was at least a cautious yes. In works such as *The Origins of Totalitarianism* (1951) and *The Life of the Mind* (1971), Arendt would argue that the systematic destruction of thought, 'the eradication of thinking in human beings, their ceasing to think for themselves, and their willingness to obey superiors who gave them orders' (Kristeva 2001:148), was at the centre of totalitarianism. Evil ultimately is 'thought defying', because 'thought tries to reach some depth, to go to the roots, and the moment it concerns itself with evil, it is frustrated because there is nothing. That is its "banality". Only the good has depth and can be radical' (Arendt 1964a:56). In linking the good with thinking, and evil with thoughtlessness or 'renouncing personal judgement', as Neiman (2002:149) expresses it, Arendt's work defends the Western philosophical tradition and its privileging of the moral significance of critical reason and the individual will. By confronting the horrors of totalitarianism and still holding on to the central goodness of critical reason, Arendt's writings are, for Neiman (2002:300), 'the best attempt at theodicy postwar philosophy has produced'. Individuals exercising critical thought may well not be enough to prevent organised or societal-wide evils surfacing again, for experience tells us that 'most people will comply' (Arendt 1963[2006]:233). However, it does mean that '*some people will not*' and '(h)umanely speaking, no more is required, and no more can reasonably be asked, for this planet to remain a place fit for human habitation' (ibid).

The implications and lessons from Arendt's writings on evil are numerous and profound. Arendt's account of Eichmann's trial shows it is not necessary for us to demonise or deny the humanity of an evil doer, even as we seek to bring them to justice (Wray-Bliss 2009). The harder and arguably far more valuable choice is to attempt to understand how humanity reproduces inhumanity, not by the process of being seduced by some radically evil Other, but through corruptions of the mundane.

> Eichmann sold his soul. Arendt's claim was not that such action was trivial but that souls generally go at bargain rates. Thirty shekels, another notch in a bureaucratic hierarchy—the things for which people are willing to betray everything that matters are appallingly insignificant.
>
> (Neiman 2002:301)

Arendt's work also reminds us that finding no 'monster' behind the commission of monstrous acts should not deflect us from so judging these acts. To use an example from earlier in this chapter, CEOs of petrochemical corporations, who prepare their companies' oil rigs for catastrophic sea level rises even while funding climate denial institutes, will almost certainly be reasonable, well mannered, articulate, affable and acting in what they consider to be their genuine fiduciary duties—and *still* they are fully morally culpable for commissioning evil. Finally, the central place that thinking has in Arendt's examination of evil means that the individual human subject and the choices that they make are never removed from her writings. The banality of Eichmann's bureaucratic evil does not in any way remove his moral culpability for the evils he commissioned and committed. His failure to think through the abhorrent consequences of his actions, or rather his failure to accord those consequences an infinitely and unassailably higher place in his thoughts and his moral considerations than his focus on his own career or narrow sense of bureaucratic duty, is still his alone.

More recent works on ethics, evil and organisations extend the arguments begun by Arendt with her observation of the banality of evil. Glover's (1999) excellent *Humanity: A Moral History of the Twentieth Century* broadens the examination of immorality in war-time conditions; in social psychology, Milgram's (1974) *Obedience to Authority: An Experimental View* and Zimbardo's *Stanford Prison Experiments* (and extension of this work in his (2008) *The Lucifer Effect*) examine the deleterious effects of authority relations and social role following behaviour on morality; Jackall's (1988) *Moral Mazes: The World of Corporate Managers*, Adams and Balfour's (1998) *Unmasking Administrative Evil* and Bauman's (1991) 'Afterthought' to his (1989) *Modernity and the Holocaust* examine the bureaucratisation of immorality in the organisational realm. In these works, as per Arendt's earlier observations, some individuals resist the pull of immorality. Jackall and Glover cite whistleblowers (on corporate malfeasance and the Mai Lai massacre respectively); Bauman documents some remarkable individual acts of resistance and self-sacrifice; and Milgram and Zimbardo observed subjects who refused the commands of authority. However, the seductions of career, the comfort of rule-following behaviour, the expectations of the social role and the focus of narrow procedural-instrumental rationality are stronger than the pull of morality for most.

With each text that carries the argument off into further territory, Arendt's caution against treating the banality of evil as a theory or doctrine, and her insistence in renewing our focus upon the central issue of individual critical thought and judgement, tends to slip a little further from sight, however. Bureaucracy, relations of authority, hierarchy, the impersonal corporation starts to morph into the form of a new Adversary, and the 'demonology of big organisations' (Parker 2002:134) is reproduced not merely by the culture industries, but by more academic critiques of the corporation. Has 'the corporation' then taken over the position of the Great Corrupter? And, if it has, could it yet be redeemed? This is the question addressed in the following chapter, where I examine the application of the theological concept of 'soul' to corporations.

# 4  Soul

Can a business have a mind? A subconscious? A knack for predicting the future? Reflexes faster than the speed of thought? Can a business have a spirit? Can a business have a soul? Can a business be alive? The answer is simple. The answer is SAP HANA.

Advertisement for relational database management system<br>SAP HANA, marketed by German Multinational<br>Software Corporation, SAP SE

Thinking of business corporations as possessing a soulful status has history. Marchand (1998) documents how, following public decrying of the soullessness of giant merged US corporations in the late nineteenth century, business leaders and their allies embarked on explicit attempts to imbue the corporation with soul. Articles and images with titles such as 'The Heart of a "Soulless Corporation"' (1908), 'Corporations and Souls' (1912), *United States Steel: A Corporation with Soul* (1921), 'Puts Flesh and Blood into "Soulless Corporation"' (1921), *Refuting the Old Idea of the Soulless Corporation* (1926), and 'Humanizing a "Soulless Corporation"' (1937) appeared in news and magazine publications. Attempts were made to import Henri Fayol's vaunted *esprit de corps* through a plethora of employee welfare policies; to imbue corporations with personality through a stream of corporate advertising that asserted 'a man talking— a man who takes pride in his accomplishments—not a soulless corporation', as early advertising expert Claude Hopkins expressed it (Marchand 1998:28); and to enlighten and improve the corporation's consumers and employees through the beautification of commercial and manufacturing premises. Corporate headquarters were remodelled and refashioned with 'architectural allusions to the sublime' (ibid:39), 'utilising ecclesiastical associations of gothic style', incorporating 'conspicuously wasted space' for symbolic towers, bells, beacons and 'grand, ennobling entrances' (Bluestone 1991, in Marchand 1998:41). Such 'honorific styling' (Milne 1981, in Marchand 1998:41) of corporate premises was intended to create a 'cathedral-like quality' (Gibbs 1984, in Marchand 1998:38) and was successful in doing so, as awed reference in the media to these cathedrals of commerce attested. The upsurge of concern with corporate soul in the early years of twentieth-century corporate America waned, however, around the 1940s, with ideas of corporate 'neighbourliness' replacing discourses of soul—a discourse which was coming to seem archaic in the modernising post-war era of the 1940s.

Five decades later, as another manifestation of the confluence of neoliberalism and religiosity, the concepts of corporate soul surfaced strongly again in the US. From the 1990s management texts conceptualised corporations in ways that sought to 'demonstrate the spiritual nature of organizations by introducing transcendent notions of authenticity, meaning, higher consciousness and purpose' (Bell, Taylor and Driscoll 2012:426). These writings were 'further strengthened by the emergence of the workplace spirituality movement' (see Ashmos and Duchon 2000; Bell and Taylor 2003, 2004; Giacalone and Jurkiewicz 2003; Mitroff and Denton 1999; Neal and Biberman 2003) and populist writers came to use the term soul 'to signify corporations that promote belief through culture, values and the actions of leaders' (ibid:426). Spanning the mid-1990s to the present, these works included titles such as *Leading with Soul: An Uncommon Journey of Spirit* (Bolman and Deal 1995), *The Soul of a Business* (Chappell 1996), *Redefining Corporate Soul: Linking Purpose and People* (Cox and Liesse 1996), *Bringing Your Soul to Work: An Everyday Practice* (Peppers and Briskin 2000), *The Soul of an Organization: Understanding the Values That Drive Successful Corporate Cultures* (Gallagher 2002), *The Soul of a Leader: Finding Your Path to Fulfilment and Success* (Benefiel 2008), *Soul Trader: Putting the Heart Back into Your Business* (Ogunlaru 2012); *The Soul of Business: How to Create and Sustain the Right Culture in Your Company* (Flowers 2014).

In some of these corporate soul texts, the religious is not drawn upon to a significant extent. For instance, in Batsone's (2003) rather lengthily titled *Saving the Corporate Soul & (Who Knows?) Maybe Your Own: Eight Principles for Creating and Preserving Integrity and Profitability without Selling Out*, soul is really little more than a synonym for corporate culture. The 'eight principles' for saving soul are familiar and secular: valuing the worker, respecting the environment, being community minded, and so on. Other texts draw more heavily upon religiously inflected discourse while still not necessarily seeking to make religion a central trope. Zenoff (2013) *The Soul of the Organization: How to Ignite Employee Engagement and Productivity at Every Level*, for instance, presents as a fairly typical culture management text, though one that uses a number of religiously inspired terms to do so. For example, we are told that 'organizations can explain, clarify, honour, glorify, elevate, emphasize, and remind employees of their most important meanings, the sources of their vitality, their essential character, and their transcendent ideals. In other words, they define anew and celebrate their souls' (ibid:104). Like many corporate soul texts, Zenoff lists organisations he has worked with that he claims have strong souls. For Zenoff these include Larkin Street Youth Services, Sisters of Mercy, Stanford University, The University of Notre Dame, San Francisco International Airport, Barclays Global Investors, Dodge and Cox, Merrill Lynch, Wells Fargo Bank, Levi Strauss and Williams-Sonoma. Other authors have their own idiosyncratic lists. Bellingham's (2009) *Creating Organizational Soul*, for example lists Google, Lotus, AT&T, Haelan Group, Homeless Solutions Inc., Somerset Hills YMCA, Visiting Nurses Association, Life University and Berkeley-Carroll Elementary School. Bellingham also provides appendixes of helpful checklists for business leaders to measure their organisational soul health, soul sickness, leadership and soulful conditions. Claims of significant performance improvements are—as in the poplar management literature more generally—standard across these soul works. For example, we are told that 'creating organizational soul has been the most important factor in achieving results across a variety of organizations. And the results are not only dramatic; they are also significantly different from the results that come out of organizations without soul' (Bellingham 2009:24).

While texts such as those above may seek to profit from association with the widespread appeal of religion in North American society, even though they do not seek to make the religious a central conceptual aspect of their work, other texts do connect Christianity and corporate soul directly. For example in *Business with Soul: Creating a Workplace Rich in Faith and Values* (2009), CEO and Chairman Michael Cardone (co-written with Mark Spuler, Chief Spiritual Officer of Cardone Industries) reminisces and evangelises on the marriage of business and Christianity that he claims to have achieved across his nationwide US automotive parts retooling business. 'Our first corporate objective' he writes, 'is to honor God. This means doing the right things, being a good steward, and caring for people' (ibid:110), and '(l)ike our automotive parts, our biblically based principles and practices have been roadtested under intense competitive pressure and in challenging business environments' (Introductory pages). The text is comprised of personal and company history, descriptions of company practices (having company chaplains and a Spiritual Life department, for example), end-of-chapter test-yourself questions for other business leaders, and vignettes concerning the employees that Cardone's Christian-soul-filled business has helped. As an example, one such vignette concerns Vicki's life. An African immigrant to the US, Vicki started on the smog-pump assembly line at Cardone in 1989. Initially, repeatedly late for work, Human Resources and the Cardone chaplains got involved and discovered that Vicki was raising two children on her own, had no car and was struggling to get them to day care on public transport before work.

> After many conversations with one of our chaplains. . . . She turned
> to God . . . (and) made the changes needed to simplify her life, help

her children, and reduce her travel time. This enabled her to refocus her efforts at work and her work performance improved.

(ibid:51)

Over the course of subsequent years, Vicki earned a degree through night school and spent her lunch hours teaching herself typing and computing. In the late 1990s she applied for an office position at Cardone, passed the skills test and was appointed. Such is an example of how Cardone's Christian business principles and soul-filled workplace saved one employee. Now, in case promoting a degree-qualified, computer literate, loyal and hard-working employee to an office position may not quite sound like this Christian soulful business is making the sort of extraordinary sacrifice that the life of Jesus is supposed to represent, Michael Cardone is clear; he is 'a realist and a capitalist, who surrounds himself with men and women who are also realists and capitalists' (ibid:14). His Christian soul-filled business is first and foremost a business, and principles of business profitability and managerial efficiency rule. Indeed, even the company chaplains and the Spiritual Life department have 'an annual budget, a strategic plan with measurable goals, and a long list of recurring activities' (p. 124).

> We link real business goals with our chaplains' objectives. Two of those goals are related to turnover/retention and absenteeism/tardiness. Our chaplains have strategies, goals, and key indicators for measuring their impact on our people indicators. As an example, in one recent year, the chaplains' annual report revealed that they impacted our business financially in these ways: 98 cases of potential terminations were reversed, saving our company $735,000.2; 6,999 cases of potential absenteeism/tardiness were eliminated, saving the company $417,345.3.
>
> (p. 131)

Proof of God's pleasure lies with the business's profitability. Cardone (p. 14) approvingly quotes Pollard's contention in (1996) *The Soul of the Firm* that 'God and business do mix, and profit is a standard for determining the effectiveness of our combined efforts'. Ultimately, this 'businessman with a soul' has 'no doubt that God uses our resources and our work at CARDONE, including our manufacturing plants, our equipment, our processes, and our products to help bring about and fulfil His purposes' (p. 36).

## Governing the Soul

In their review and critique of corporate soul texts such as those above, Bell, Taylor and Driscoll (2012) observed that they performed a largely normative function. Like Michael Cardone's confident self-assurance that his business and God's purposes align, corporate soul writings can be seen as 'cheerleading' (Giacalone 2010) for business and the strong guidance of business leaders. By deploying the concept to reassure us that big business is full of goodness (and God), corporate soul might seem like a barren idea for critical scholars of organisation. The temptation then may be to avoid this space and leave the discourse of organisational soul to the apologists and evangelists of capital. I think it would be a mistake to do so. The concept of soul is such a rich and redolent one in our cultures and histories that we might instead do better to heed Nietzsche's admonishment: 'we do not need to get "rid of the soul" itself nor do without one of our oldest, most venerable hypotheses . . . the way is clear for new and refined versions of the hypothesis about the soul' (Nietzsche 1886[2006]:317). Rather than abandon it to those who use it to legitimise business and co-opt Christianity further into this cause, we can instead engage in some further soul-searching; to see how this 'venerable hypothesis' might enable further critique of corporations.

In actuality, soul—not of corporations but rather of their individual human members—has been engaged with within critical social science studies for some time. In *Discipline and Punish: The Birth of the Prison* (1975[1995]), Michel Foucault wrote what he intended to be a contribution to a 'history of the modern soul' (ibid:23). He traced the shift in Europe from physical punishment and torture-based penal systems to an increasingly non-corporeal one that 'acts in depth on the heart, the thoughts, the will, the inclinations' such that '(t)he apparatus of punitive justice must now bite into this bodiless reality' (ibid:16–17). Through the extension of judges' power of examination, through the inclusion of experts on psychology and pathology in the judicial process and through intricate systems of surveillance and discipline in penal institutions, the legal system laid hold 'not only on offences, but on individuals; not only on what they do, but also on what they are, will be, may be . . . namely the "soul" of the criminal' (ibid:18–19). This soul was 'born out of methods of punishment, supervision and constraint' meaning that the soul 'is the effect and instrument of a political anatomy; the soul is the prison of the body' (ibid:29–30). The use of the term 'soul' in Foucault's work to refer to those psychological, spiritual and moral depths of being that modern individuals are compelled to have and through which we are governed should not be understood simply as rhetorical flourish. As Foucault insisted, soul is real.

> It would be wrong to say that the soul is an illusion, or an ideological effect. On the contrary, it exists, it has a reality, it is a product permanently around, on, within the body by the functioning of power that is exercised on those punished—and, in a more general way, on those one supervises, trains and corrects, over madmen, children at home

and at school, the colonized, over those who are stuck at a machine and supervised for the rest of their lives.

(Foucault 1975[1995]:29)

Such an understanding that power is typically exercised in modern societies not as the imposition of an alien force—like torture or domination—but rather through our subjectivity or souls, has become a central idea of contemporary social science. Rose's (1989, 1999) *Governing the Soul*, for example, extended the empirical scope of Foucault's ideas to consider the hand that 'our contemporary "engineers of the human soul"' (1999: xxii), the psychological sciences, had played to 'fabricate subjects—human men, women and children—capable of bearing the burdens of liberty' (ibid:viii). '(T)he management of subjectivity has become a central task for the modern organization', wrote Rose, and organisations 'have come to fill the space between the "private" lives of citizens and the "public" concerns of rulers' (ibid:2). This concern with the ways that organisations are governing through appealing to and shaping the 'private' subjectivities of their members flowed into the organisation studies cannon, and a substantial body of work has been produced examining this (e.g. Bardon and Josserand 2011; Collinson 1994; Grey 1994; Kelly, Allender and Colquhoun 2007; Knights 1990; Knights and Willmott 1989; Knights and Vurdubakis 1994; McCabe 2000; Miller and O'Leary 1987; Roberts et al. 2006; Rose 1991; Skinner 2013; Spence and Rinaldi 2014; Walker 2010). And, while much of the above work has tended to substitute the theologically sanitised term 'subject' for the original 'soul', it should be noted that for Foucault and Nietzsche these terms were interchangeable (for example, Nietzsche 1887[2007]:27).

From such works, and both Foucault's and Nietzsche's original insights, we understand the soul or subjectivity of individual organisational members to be governed and disciplined, and for this to be a central means through which power is exercised in modern society. But what about the soul or subject of the corporation itself? Can it be similarly governed or disciplined? Perhaps it might. Judith Butler, for example, argues that 'the subject' is not the originating source from which something like morality stems—a construction criticised by Nietzsche as the atomistic Christian conceptualisation of innate and immortal soul (1886[2006]). Rather the subject is 'the effect of power in recoil' (Butler 1997:6). That is, the moral subject is not a *precondition* of morality. On the contrary, it is moralising and disciplinary practices which bring into existence the subject. The subject is a political effect; it is that which is *subjected to* moral, disciplinary practices. As Butler writes,

'(t)he subject' is sometimes bandied about as if it were interchangeable with 'the person' or 'the individual'. The genealogy of the subject as a critical category, however, suggests that the subject, rather than be identified strictly with the individual, ought to be designated as a linguistic category, a place holder, a structure in formation.

(Butler 1997:10)

By differentiating the 'subject' from the categories 'person' or 'individual', we might begin to conceptualise other 'structures in formation'—possibly even such structures as corporations—occupying a subject or soulful status; one that can be disciplined and governed. Before we get ahead of ourselves, however, is there anything in the history of soul that suggests that the concept can be applied to something such as a corporation?

## On Human and Non-Human Souls

Diverse concepts of soul surface within different religious and historical periods. Even limiting ourselves to Western traditions, there is great variety—with several accounts receptive to supra- or non-human manifestations of soul. As Santoro et al. (2009:634) observe in their review of the anatomic location of soul, published in the journal *Neurosurgery*, 'the soul has been described as being localized in a specific organ or anatomic structure, or as being nonlocalized in any organ or structure and, in some instances, as being trans-human and even pan-cosmological'.

Christian conceptualisations of soul have Neoplatonic roots, particularly with respect to the immortality of soul and the importance of reason regulating the body. Plato's own ideas on soul, however, were complex and varied. The soul was a prisoner of the body, to be set free (*Phaedo*). It was a hierarchy of levels and functions which, like the republic itself, must be ordered and harmonised for it to aspire to justice (*Republic*, see Foucault 2005:55). It was a multiply-natured essence—rational, spirited/impulsive, and desiring/appetitive—located in the brain, thorax and abdomen respectively (Santoro et al. 2009). Continuing long-held Greek ideas, soul was also that which animated life, with the implication (somewhat tacit in Socrates, though explicit later in Aristotle) that all things that are alive, not just humans, had souls. Indeed, the earlier Greek scholar Thales mused upon whether even magnets may have souls, given that magnets can move iron, and it is the distinctive characteristic of living things to be able to initiate movement (Lorenz 2009). Perhaps most poetically of Plato's characterisations, the human soul was a pair of winged horses, one dark and recalcitrant, one light and obedient, pulling a chariot steered by a charioteer (*Phaedo*). It was the task of the charioteer (reason) to harness the (desiring) dark and (spirited) light aspects of soul so as to achieve harmony. Here, as Santoro et al. (2009:636) observe:

Plato's tripartite theory of the soul finds a structural-functional similarity with Freud's tripartite theory of the ego, id, and superego, with the ego representing the rational principle that seeks to harmonize the primitive demands of the id, representing the instinctual or spirited impulses of the body, and that of the superego, representing the internalized moral-social demands of society.

Such resonance between a modernist, psychological understanding of the subject and a classical conceptualisation of the soul are not coincidental. The Greek soul, *psuchē*, is the etymological root of 'psyche', the basis of all our present *psy*-terms, and the pre-eminence of Plato's rational soul as the orchestrating force was carried forward through Christianity, the Enlightenment and into the still-dominant Cartesian conceptualisation of mind as defining human self and action (Matthews 1992). However, even in Plato's *encephalocentric* (brain-centred) conceptualisations, soul was always more than rational 'mind' alone (Lorenz 2009), having for instance the qualities of immortality, the association with justice and ethics, and being the animating basis of life itself.

While Neoplatonic understandings of the immortality of the soul were carried into the Christian religion, Plato's ideas on soul were far from the last word in Classical Greek culture. In his *The Soul of the Greeks* (2011:2), Davis argues that from 'the very first sentence of their first and most famous poem', Homer's *Iliad*, the importance of soul for the Greeks is apparent:

> Sing, Goddess, Achilles' rage,
> Black and murderous, that cost the Greeks,
> Incalculable pain, pitched countless souls,
> Of heroes into Hades' dark,
> And left their bodies to rot as feasts,
> For dogs and birds, as Zeus' will was done.

Concern with the soul was carried through the works of other major Greek scholars—including Herodotus, Euripides, Plato, Socrates, Pythagoras, Parmenides and Democritus (Davis 2011; Lorenz 2009; Santoro et al. 2009). It was, however, Plato's most famous student, Aristotle, who produced the most 'direct and nonancillary' discussion of soul amongst the Greeks (Davis 2011:9). Aristotle's *De Animus* (Latin for 'On Soul', or more literally, 'that which animates', translated from the Greek title *Peri Psuchēs*, 'about soul') was a work which both continued and departed from Plato's conceptualisation of soul in important respects. For Aristotle, soul is that which animates life—*all* life. Aristotle differentiated nutritive soul, from sensing soul, from cognitive or thinking soul, with the primary activity of a living thing being that which constitutes its soul. Where plant life was nutritive soul, and animal life consisted of both nutritive and sensing soul, humans alone were animated by nutritive, sensing and thinking soul. Inseparable as it was from the life of the organism itself, soul was material and mortal and did not survive or function after the death of the body. With his privileging of soul as embodied, mortal and animating life,

Aristotle's conceptualisation would come to inform a *cadiocentric* theory of the soul, one where the heart is understood as animating the body (Santoro et al. 2009), as distinct from Plato's *encephalocentric* views. Together these two different understandings of soul—Plato's immortal, immaterial, and Aristotle's mortal, material, soul—would largely define most subsequent understandings in the West (Santoro et al. 2009; Sutton 2013).

Notwithstanding their differences, both Plato and Aristotle held to a trichotomic view of soul (Plato's two, desiring and spirited winged horses and the reasoning charioteer, as we have seen above, and Aristotle's nutritive, sensing and rational soul). Legacies of a trichotomic view can be found in Christian writings—for example the person understood as constituting rational soul (*psyche*), body (*soma*) and spirit (*pneuma*), and in the idea of the Holy Trinity, comprising God, the Son and the Holy Spirit. Finer distinctions between two elements of this tripartite—rational soul (*psyche*) and spirit (*pneuma*)—collapsed somewhat within the New Testament, such that Homeric terms normally translated as spirit or 'breath of life' (Davis 2011:9) morphed into an interchangeable use of spirit/soul in the Christian text. This foreshadowed a subsequent marginalisation of the soul-as-spirit in favour of a dominant conceptualisation of rational, human-centric soul, modelled upon a bipartite view of the person as consisting of body and soul (Mendelson 2012).

If, however, we draw back for a moment from this later domination of rational soul and consider the long-held connection of soul/spirit, we see further possibilities for conceptualising soul in supra-human ways. *Pneuma*, translated as 'spirit' (and 'breath'—hence pneumatic and other terms associated with the force of air), may be thought of as the inspiration, or the muse, that blows into us from outside. It is 'irredeemably exterior' and is 'not related . . . to a free will or to a subject that controls its life in an independent way' even though it may 'fill the interior' (Kaulingfreks and ten Bos 2001:4 and 5). The products of human creativity and inspiration can carry soul-as-spirit onwards. Even our published writing

> become(s) almost human . . . it goes about finding its readers, kindles life, pleases, horrifies, fathers new works, becomes the soul of others' resolutions and behaviour. In short, it lives like a being fitted out with a mind and soul—yet it is nevertheless not human.
>
> (Nietzsche 1878[2006]:179)

This spirit may be more collective too in its effects, representing 'a profound aspect of human togetherness' (Kaulingfreks and ten Bos 2001:4). The German translation of spirit, *geist*, is a term well used in social science and philosophy to refer to the defining and animating quality of supra-human collectives. Weber's use of *geist* in his (1930[2001]) *Die protestantische Ethik und der Geist des Kapitalismus* to conceptualise the animating and defining life-force of capitalist society is well established—and emulated (Blanchard 2010; Boltanski and Chiapello 1999[2005]; Campbell 2005; Greenfeld 2001; Novak 1982, 1993; Stiegler 2006[2014]). This in turn draws upon a longer history of examining the *zeitgeist*, flowing back most notably to Hegel who in his (1807[1977]) *Phänomenologie des Geistes* and (1806) *Philosophie des Geistes* sought to identify the spirits of different historic-cultural periods and their contributions to the ever-advancing development of World-Spirit.

Even from the above brief review of a small number of sources in the Western tradition, we can say that there are significant religious, historical and philosophical works that do not, by fiat, exclude conceptualisations of soul as applicable to non-human or supra-human entities. We have encountered plant soul, animal soul, immortal soul, soul as separate from the body, soul as spirit, spirit existing outside the person, and spirit defining a times, a collective, an economic system, even the flow of world history. Perhaps most tellingly, however, for the possibility of intelligibly applying a theological conceptualisation of soul to a supra-human collective such as an organisation, might be the pronouncement of a modern Christian authority: His Holiness John Paul II. In his *General Audience* of July 1988, entitled 'The Holy Spirit: Soul of the Church', John Paul II was most explicit that the organisation we call the Church has a soul. 'The Holy Spirit dwells in the Church not as a guest who still remains an outsider, but as the soul that transforms the community into "God's holy temple" (1 Cor 3:17; cf. 6:19; Eph 2:21)'. John Paul II cites numerous other Christian authorities in support of his view, including his predecessor Leo XIII ('If Christ is the Head of the Church, the Holy Spirit is her soul'), Aurelius Augustine ('What our spirit, i.e., our soul, is for our members, the Holy Spirit is for Christ's members, for the Body of Christ which is the Church' Serm. 267, 4), the Second Vatican Ecumenical Council (Christ 'has shared with us his Spirit who, being one and the same in head and members, gives life to, unifies and moves the whole body. Consequently, his work could be compared by the Fathers to the function that the principle of life, the soul, fulfils in the human body' Lumen gentium, n. 7) and St Gregory of Nyssa ('surrounded by the unity of the Holy Spirit as the bond of peace, all will be one Body and one Spirit' Hom. 15 in Cant.).

## Reconceptualising Corporate Soul

If a human collective such as a church can be understood to have soul, what about a corporation? Well, if we start first with the translation of soul as 'subject', a body of previous work has sought to conceptualise corporations as having a subject status in their own right. These have included arguments that corporations are moral subjects because they exercise moral agency (Arnold 2006; Moore 1999; Soares 2003), have moral personhood (French 1979; Phillips 1992), have a conscience (Goodpaster and Matthews 1982) or demonstrate intentionality (French

2014). By conceptualising the corporation as a moral subject, an appeal can be made to these subjects to exercise responsibility through voluntary acts of ethical agency, and such writings have provided key conceptual support for practices such as corporate social responsibility. The voluntarism and appeal to corporate conscience which developments such as CSR would seem to entail, however, have been problematised by critical organisational scholars (e.g. Banerjee 2007; Bevan and Corvellec 2007; Jones 2003; Jones, Parker and ten Bos 2005; Parker 2002; Roberts 2001, 2003). Lampert (2016), for example, considers such constructions as an attempt 'to address *morally* problems which are better addressed *politically*' (Lampert 2016:99). He traces this mistake directly back to the ideas of a corporate moral subject status at their core: 'it is a mistake to think of (or treat) corporations as moral agents, and that CSR's impotency is a direct result of this mistake' (Lampert 2016:79).

Some explicitly critical works though have sought to articulate a strong critique of corporations while framing this critique within a conceptualisation of corporate subjecthood. Bakan's (2004) *The Corporation* is perhaps the most well known of these and takes us through the steps through which 'by the end of the nineteenth century . . . the courts had fully transformed the corporation into a "person"' (ibid:16). For Bakan, however, these are persons that demonstrate a particular pathology. They are subjects that relentlessly pursue their own selfish interests and lack the constraining voice of moral conscience. They are for Bakan, in other words, psychopaths. As psychopaths, however, these corporate subjects are beyond help or redemption, lost to a pathology which has no cure. However, the story may not have to end there. Though unexplored by Bakan, the term psychopath itself originates in the longer history of soul, derived as it is from *psyche* (soul) and *pathos* (suffering/sickness). To deploy the term 'psychopath' to characterise the subjecthood of the corporation is thus already to evoke the older theological concept, *soul*. What is more, exploring a theologically informed conceptualisation of corporate soul may help us out of the impasse of irredeemable corporate pathology that Bakan's corporation-as-psychopath leaves us at.

How might theological sources be used to enable us to conceptualise corporate soul in a critical manner? One way is to draw analogy between the corporation of today and description of problematic souls presented in classical religious texts. I present such an analogy here by considering the description of Late Roman imperial soul by Early Christian scholar and Bishop of Northern African province, Hippo, Aurelius Augustine. Augustine is one of the most significant Church Fathers, a figure vital to the development of Christian thought and Western subjectivity. His writing was 'the greatest single influence on Western theology for the next thousand years' (Siedentop 2014:110) and a major force responsible for the merging of the Greek philosophical tradition—particularly that of Neoplatonism—with early Judeo-Christian religion (Mendelson 2012). His *Confessions* (400[1961]), which I consider later, is one of, if not *the*, first hermeneutics of the subject (Coles 1992), prefiguring the West's radical break from imperial Roman to Christian subjectivity. However, it is Augustine's depiction of the imperial Roman subject of Late Antiquity in *The City of God* (written between 413 and 427 CE, a time of profound crisis for the Roman Empire) that may be seen as analogous for the soul of the corporation today.

For Augustine the imperial Roman subject, like our modern corporation, was defined by a 'lust' for domination (427[1972]:104), power (ibid:42) and the valorisation of imperial conquest, resulting in a 'seemingly endless tale of subjugation' (Coles 1992:17). Augustine's Roman subject was rapacious. It was not one in search of a modest existence, a comfortable, sustainable materiality from which a morality of self-restraint could be exercised. Rather, like the profit-seeking corporation, it was a subject whose prosperity only 'depraved' it further (Augustine 427[1972]:45) such that it sought ever more extreme ways to exercise its insatiable lust for glory, sensation and domination. Liberty, when achieved by these subjects, as too under neoliberal policy today, resulted not in respectful coexistence. Rather it manifested itself in the desire for sovereignty (p. 42), understood as the desire to reduce relations with others to those of domination and subjugation. 'For when can the lust for power in arrogant hearts come to rest until after passing from one office to another, it arrives at sovereignty?' (p. 42). Augustine's Roman subject commits the core, ontological sin of pride—of believing itself to be its own self-originating light and living only by the 'rule of self' (p. 552)—and thereby seeks to renounce its relations of reciprocity, responsibility and reliance upon others, the world and, for Augustine, God the creator (Coles 1992:16). We have then the depiction of a subject to whom liberty is the domination and subjugation of others, and prosperity engenders further depravity. 'But when liberty had been won, "such a passion for glory took hold of them" that liberty alone did not satisfy—they had to acquire dominion' (Augustine 427[1972]:198, quoting Roman historian and critic, Sallust). Such a subject, as Augustine depicted it, had no regard for the intrinsic value of others or the world. For while 'it is the nature of things considered in itself, without regard to our convenience or inconvenience, that gives glory to the Creator' (p. 476), the lustful self values only such things which bring it glory.

At times such subjects, as with our neoliberal corporations, could display a semblance of public morality. But such public morality was not produced by virtue *of* virtue. Rather—and here we might see resonance with the emergence of CSR and the like at those points in history where corporations have faced the effects of a wider legitimation crisis—it was a restraint born of fear. Referencing Sallust again, Augustine observes that:

> He records the high standards of morality and the degree of concord
> which marked the history of Rome between the Second Punic War

and the last, but he ascribes as the reason for the desirable state of things not the love of justice, but the fear that peace was unreliable while Carthage still stood; and that was why Nasica resisted the annihilation of Carthage, so that wickedness should be restrained by fear, immorality checked, and the high standards of conduct preserved.

(Augustine 427[1972]:68)

Without the constraining hand of fear, when opposition was vanquished, the 'height of excellence' soon descends again to the 'depth of depravity' (p. 69). Thus, in a passage which evokes contemporary critiques of global business practices—such as Arundhati Roy's (2014) powerful descriptions of land-clearing and village-razing in India—when the corporation is beyond the constraining juridical eye of 'developed' countries or concerned consumers,

> the patricians reduced the plebeians to the condition of slavery; they disposed of the lives and the persons of the plebs in the manner of kings; they drove men from their lands; and with the rest of the people disenfranchises, they alone wielded supreme power.
>
> (Sallust in Augustine 427[1972]:68)

Paralleling perhaps the global financial crisis, where corporations threatened each other's very existence in orgies of deregulated market behaviour, Augustine notes how in the absence of countervailing and limiting fear,

> the degradation of traditional morality ceased to be a gradual decline and became a torrential downhill rush. The young were so corrupted by luxury and greed that it was justly observed that a generation had arisen which could neither keep its own property or allow others to keep theirs.
>
> (Sallust in Augustine 427[1972]:69)

Not even the prospect of 'their country's overthrow' (read the sacking of Rome or, indeed, a US—even global—financial crisis) could correct their vices (p. 44).

## Writing on the Soul

If, as I have suggested, Augustine's depiction of the imperial Roman subject of Late Antiquity is analogous to the soul of the business corporation, what does this offer us? What this theologically informed conceptualisation offers is the tantalising possibility of corporate soul's redemption. Augustine's writings punctuated a period marked by a profound transformation of moral subjectivity—from that of the Classical Roman soul to the emergence and eventual dominance in the West of the confessing, self-interrogating soul of Christianity (Foucault 2005). Where the Christian subject was to be preoccupied with a continual and permanent hermeneutics of the self, an inward-looking questioning of the self as something to be 'renounced', 'deciphered' and 'constantly examined because in this self were lodged concupiscence and desires of the flesh' (Foucault 1984:366), the Roman subject was concerned with quite a different *telos* or end, organised around the mastery and management of the self:

> one must manage oneself as a governor manages the governed, as a head of an enterprise manages his enterprise, a head of household manages his household . . . virtue consists essentially in perfectly governing oneself, that is, in exercising upon oneself as exact a mastery as that of a sovereign against whom there would no longer be revolts.
>
> (Foucault 1984:363)

These two different soulful positions—that of the self-renouncing, self-interrogating Christian and the self-mastering Roman—were constituted through a variety of disciplinary practices, from fasting, meditation, prayer, the keeping of diaries, withdrawal from the world, sacrifices, disciplined remembering, exercise, abstinence, practices of purification, listening to truth and truth telling. Of all the technologies of the self available to and required of early Christian people, however, confession was arguably most defining—and most central too to the constitution of subsequent wider Western subjectivity (Foucault 1978). Here again I turn to Augustine, this time to his foundational articulation of the Christian confession, before contrasting this with the Roman practice of *hypomnemata*.

Augustine (400[1961]) considered confessing to be the fundamental ethical practice through which a being—by a disciplined and continuous practice of remembering—faces themselves and the harms they have produced and thus begins to become an ethical subject. Augustine's reflections on the 'awe-inspiring', 'profound' and 'incalculable complexity' (p. 223) of memory are well evidenced in Book Ten of *Confessions*. However, it is the meticulous articulation of personal memory in the preceding chapters of that text which represents one of the most intricate and earliest embodiments of the constitutive moral practice of the confessional in Western culture.

For Augustine, a non-confessing subject is one that exists 'behind' its 'own back' and that refuses to see itself (p. 169). It is a subject that has 'turned a blind eye' and 'forgotten' itself (ibid). Augustine regards the Roman subject as just such a figure, a flat subject, so mired in its own desires that others and the world itself are also flattened

> to the singular dimension of lust as it strives to conquer a world that invites . . . that the self subjugate it. And at the same time the subject is flattened, it is crushed and dispersed into as many objects as it desires.
>
> (Coles 1992:21)

Remembering the harms or sins one has occasioned and, crucially, publically declaring these brings the subject 'face to face' with itself (Augustine 400[1961]:169), such that it stands 'naked before my own eyes, while my conscience upbraided me' (p. 169). The disciplined act of remembering and confessing creates a moral and hermeneutic depth which is in sharp distinction to the flatness of a self-regarding, imperialist subject (p. 207). 'Oh Lord, I am working hard in this field, and the field of my labours is my own self. I have become a problem to myself . . . I am investigating myself, my memory, my mind' (p. 223). This moral work, while concerned with the subject and its memories, is also a public practice. That is, while his God knows in advance everything and does not profit from the telling, the Augustine's confession and the practice which this models for others takes the form of a public declaration. It does so precisely so as to connect the soul—which through remembering sees that it was never a unified, coherent or sovereign subject—further still with others. In Augustine's *Confessions*, for example, he writes of a profound realisation that he is a dependent being: dependent first, to an incalculable degree, upon his mother who gave life to him and raised him; dependent later upon so many others, both those who guided him and befriended him, but dependent and responsible too to those he wronged, stole from, hurt and abandoned; and dependent always on his God, who he understands to be the ground and origin of all being (Coles 1992). For Augustine, in seeking to answer the self-asked question 'Who are you?' (p. 212) through the disciplined act of remembering and confessing, one becomes a self-questioning and self-problematising subject; a subject that does not consider itself sovereign; that comes to know itself as dependent, beholden and responsible; that questions and requestions itself in the light of its deepening awareness of wrongs it has occasioned; that becomes ultimately a moral subject, with a Christian soul.

The fundamental importance of the confession in the development of the Christian (and subsequently more general Western) soul, is underlined in Foucault writings. Despite the protestant Reformation and the 'great rejection of the Catholic confessional practices' (Foucault 1984:368) in the sixteenth century, the confessional remained 'quite decisive for the genealogy of the modern self' (Foucault 1993:210), 'an absolutely crucial moment in the history of subjectivity in the West' (Foucault 1984:364), so much so that the West became and remains a 'singularly confessing society',

> The confession has spread its effects far and wide. It plays a part in justice, medicine, education, family relationships, and love relations, in the most ordinary affairs of everyday life, and in the most solemn rites; one confesses one's crimes, one's sins, one's thoughts and desires, one's illnesses and troubles; one goes about telling, with the greatest precision, whatever is most difficult to tell. One confesses in

public and in private, to one's parents, one's educators, one's doctor, to those one loves; one admits to oneself, in pleasure and pain, things it would be impossible to tell to anyone else, the things people write books about. . . . Western man [*sic*] has become a confessing animal.

(Foucault 1978:59)

If the confession was the defining technology through which the early Christian and subsequently generalised Western soul was inscribed, a parallel technology for writing the Roman soul of Late Antiquity was the *hypomnemata*. The *hypomnemata* (in Greek, *hupomnēnata*) were collections of notes that subjects made from their readings, conversations, lessons from their masters and lectures they attended. They functioned as aides-memoires, enabling the subject to memorise important things that had been said (Foucault 2005). The purpose of such notes was to enable the management and consolidation of the self—to affix to the self the remembered words and logos of authority, so as to manage the soul in the light of the already said. 'The ancients carried on this politics of themselves with these notebooks just as governments and those who manage enterprises administered by keeping registers' (Foucault 1984:363–364). The function of these self-constituting written practices was quite different to the later, inward-focussed Christian confessional. The Christian subject's 'obligation to tell the truth about himself . . . did not exist at all in Greek, Hellenistic, or Roman Antiquity' (1984:364). The function of the *hypomnemata*

is not to bring the *arcana conscientiae* to light, the confession of which—be it oral or written—has a purifying value. The movement that they seek to effect is the inverse of this last one. The point is not to pursue the indescribable, not to reveal the hidden, not to say the non-said, but, on the contrary, to collect the already-said.

(ibid 1984:365)

Through documentation of words of authority, the Roman subject would seek to perfect self by an outward-focussed process, not an inward-focussed gaze. The Roman telos is to become a subject of veridiction (Foucault 2005:362), that is, a subject or soul which is oriented to an already written truth.

## Disciplining Corporate Soul

What then might these two important technologies for writing-souls-into-being—the Roman *hypomnemata* and the Christian confession—have to say about the soul of the modern corporation?

Well, first they may tell us something about what is being constructed when corporations routinely present themselves in terms of a generalised and aspirational good: the claims to excellence; inspirational mission statements; the declaration of laudable moral, environmental and fiduciary standards; high-minded ethics policies; and assertions of corporate social responsibility. These kinds of articulations constitute the major volume of corporations' representation of an ethical subject status to its varied stakeholders. They form too the foundation of corporations' claims to being an organisation that is 'governing with soul'. Considering the above discussion of the two foundational forms of writing souls into being, though, what kind of soul might we understand as being represented and constituted through such practices? I suggest that what we *do not* see here is the kind of internally problematising, self-berating introspection redolent of a Christian confessional. Corporate proclamations of goodness do not voice a continual and ongoing self-examination of corporate behaviour—a live account which changes and responds to the 'temptations, struggles, falls, and victories' (Foucault 1984:365) that befall the corporation. The mission statement, the ethical policy and the like are, to borrow Levinas' (1998) terms, not the 'saying' of an inter-subjective relationship with another subject, a relationship that functions to undermine the corporation's claim to sovereignty. There is no other subject here to which the corporation is responding—no subject rather than the corporation's own idealised, aspirational self. As Roberts (2001:123) has argued, such claims to corporate social responsibility may be understood rather as acts of narcissism,

> managed almost exclusively at the level of appearances—through making more of what is already being done. The problem is conceived as being purely presentational, and what ensues are publications that advertise the work of the corporation in relation to the environment and associated social projects.

Even reading ethical branding, CSR and the like as more than cynical attempts at impression management they perhaps, at best, represent a collection of idealised aspirations of what the corporation might wish to be. Like *hypomnemata*, they are the 'already-said' of collected-together aphorisms and well-crafted statements rather than the anxiety of inward introspection and self-critique. Corporate proclamations of goodness seem analogous then to the technology formative in the constitution of the imperialist self-aggrandising subjectivity of Augustine's pre-Christian Romans. The soul that is being created through corporations' articulations of their own goodness and, indeed, *soulfulness* would seem to be the kind of imperialist soul not wished for in the West for its human subjects for the last two millennia.

If a corporation's articulation of generalised aspirational ethical goals, responsibilities and missions can be understood as the stuff of an imperialist subjectivity constructed though the language of ethics, what of those other ethico-political responses that may be drawn from the corporation by the actions and accusations of others? Here I am thinking of corporate responses to specific accusations of harm—accusations, for example, from the courts, from the media, from campaigners, consumers or employees. It is here, in this space where the political force of critique compels a response from the corporation, that I suggest we can see the possible beginnings of a less imperialist corporate soul. Of course, corporation's response to specific accusations of harm can vary significantly—from outright denials to some form of acknowledgement—and the ethico-political implications of these would seem to vary too. The former, the denial of responsibility for occasioning harm, would include such things as the press release denial; the defence against legal or community accusations of wrongdoing; the defamation or libel case brought by the organisation against the activist or critic; or the words used to refuse accountability and responsibility for malfeasance, for pollution, for sweatshop labour or exploitation. These sorts of corporate denials of responsibility could seem an unlikely place to look for any possibility of an ethical relationship or compassionate soul. Certainly, forthright denials of harm cannot be easily reconciled with a soul-searching Augustinian confessional. Such denial lacks the self-berating inversion of the other's accusation into the substance of the self which Nietzsche regarded as formative for the development of 'bad conscience' (Nietzsche 1887[2007]). Notwithstanding, corporate denials of responsibility may still be regarded as doing something in ethical terms that confident proclamations of corporate goodness do not. That is, they *respond*. As Butler (2005) observes, even when they are denied, in responding to the accusations levelled by others, a subject begins to constitute itself as accountable to the other. That is, the subject begins to deconstruct the claim to an imperious (and imperial) sovereignty.

> I have been addressed, even perhaps had an act attributed to me, and a certain threat of punishment backs up this interrogation . . . [and] I begin my story of myself only in the face of a 'you' who asks me to give an account.
>
> (p. 11)

In not remaining silent, where silence 'attempts to circumscribe a domain of autonomy that cannot or should not be intruded upon by the questioner' (p. 12), a response 'must, from the outset, accept the possibility that the self has causal agency, even if, in a given instance, the self may not have been the cause of the suffering in question' (p. 12). A denial is still a response and in so responding we can see early groundwork for the beginnings of an ethical encounter and the undoing of imperial corporate soul.

Such beginnings of an ethical encounter would seem most significant, however, in those instances when a corporation acknowledges its occasioning of harm: the apology, the legal acceptance of fault, the monies paid in reparation, the *mea culpa*. It is in these instances that I suggest we can see the opening a practice which begins to approach the disciplinary act of the confession: that is, a public remembering and declaration of harms occasioned to others, one through which a subject acknowledges its dependence upon and relationship with those others, and thereby sets up possible conditions for the remembering of the same in the future. What though of the fact that acknowledgement of harm is likely forced upon the corporation by the external pressure of legal judgements, public outrage, activist pressure or government censure rather than an act of voluntary contrition? Does this, the imposed violence of the other's critique, rather than the spontaneous outpourings of a contrite soul, fatally undermine analogy to the soul-constituting practice of the confession? It might do if we regard confession, and the formation of morality more generally, as necessarily voluntary and other to violence. Such an understanding, however, may be hard to sustain. Augustine himself, as Coles (1992:31) notes, speaks of becoming a confessing subject as 'the most traumatic experience of his life'. The long history of confessions—their intimate association with the violence of torture, threat, fear and death—including, if not especially, in Judeo-Christian cultures, shows the idea of the purely voluntary confession to be rather a quaint notion. More broadly, for Nietzsche (in *On the Genealogy of Morality* and *Beyond Good and Evil*) and Freud (in *On the Mechanism of Paranoia*, *Totem and Taboo*, *On Narcissism* and *Civilization and Its Discontents*), violence is not the other to morality. It is its constitutive basis. Morality or conscience represents the subject turning back upon itself the violence of a prohibition or the excising of a desire.

> When man decided he had to make a memory for himself, it never happened without blood, torments and sacrifices . . . all this has its origin in that particular instinct which discovered that pain was the most powerful aid to mnemonics . . . with the aid of such images and procedures, man was eventually able to retain five or six 'I-don't-want-to's' in his memory . . . what a price had to be paid for them! how much blood and horror lies at the basis of 'all good things'!
>
> (Nietzsche 1887[2007:38–39])

Foucault carried the conceptualisation of violence-constituted morality into *Madness and Civilisation* (1965[1988]), *Discipline and Punish* (1975[1995]) and *The History of Sexuality* (1978), demonstrating how '(w)hen it is not spontaneous or dictated by some internal imperative, the confession is wrung from a person by violence or threat; it is driven from its hiding place in the soul, or extracted from the body' (Foucault 1978:59), whether this is by blasting the mentally ill with cold water until they confess to delusions (1963[1994]) or underlining regicidal confessions through the use of hanging, drawing and quartering (1975[1995]). Even the work of that most compassionate of ethicists, Levinas, is replete with images of ethics as the violent destabilising of a sovereign self. Ethics is understood as the unbidden persecution and invasion of the self by the other; it is depicted as being 'commanded', 'held hostage', 'stripped naked', 'compelled', exposed to 'traumas' and 'wounding'; it is 'pain' (Levinas 1974[1988]). Taking the above together, not only is 'morality predicated on a certain kind of violence' but 'such violence founds the subject' (Butler 1997:64). A power *exerted on* a subject' is nevertheless also 'a power *assumed by* the subject, an assumption that constitutes the instrument of that subject's becoming' (ibid:11). In forcing a corporation to acknowledge its occasioning of harm, we can see the beginning of a concerted undermining of an extant imperial corporate soul—the possibility of corporations being 'turned to face themselves from behind their own backs' (Augustine 400[1961]), compelled into depth from a flat morality of self-interest (Coles 1992) and brought to a position where they acknowledge relationships of dependency and responsibility.

## Body and Soul

'Corporation', from the Latin *corporare*, means to form into a body. I have argued that this body has a soul. Treating this body as ensouled is not a semantic trick. From my reading of early and more recent Christian theology, Classical Greek philosophy, and social scientific and philosophical work concerned with spirit or *geist*, the term 'soul' may be applied to corporations. I argue this is not to imply that 'cheerleading' pronouncements of soul-filled organisations should now replace critics' long-favoured denouncing of corporations as 'soulless leviathans'. Nor still does it seek to replicate the kind of conceptualisations of corporate moral personhood and corporate moral agency that have been charged with providing philosophical foundations for a voluntarist CSR. Instead, the exploration of corporate soul that I have presented here reminds us that soul is by no means reducible to the modernist ideal of an autonomous, sovereign subject: whether this subject is corporeal *or* corporate. The soul is conditioned, constructed, *disciplined*. It is as much or more a product from *without*—a product of forced confession, punishment or violence (Levinas 1998; Foucault 1963[1994], 1975[1995]; Nietzsche 1887[2007])—as it ever was one of calm and quiet self-directed introspection. Much as the 'turn to ethics' in literary studies, philosophy and political theory over the last 20 years was engendered by a radical decentring of the (human) subject—a decentring that enabled critical scholars to engage with the ethical without having to reproduce problematic discourses of autonomy and sovereignty (Garber, Hanssen and Walkowitz 2000; see, for example, the collection by Cadava, Connor and Nancy 1991). The examination of corporate soul that I have presented here enables us to work with ideas of corporate subject status while decentring the corporation as the author of its own ethics. Ascribing to corporations a soul does not necessitate waiting around for their voluntary contrition or spontaneous outpourings of conscience, social responsibility and philanthropy. Rather, it underlines the importance of continual ethico-political practices that discipline these souls, that force them to account for and confess to harms, so that they may be wrenched from a state of neoliberal sovereignty, a place almost 'beyond good and evil', and instead, to paraphrase Nietzsche (1887[1996]:63), frightened back into themselves and given an inner life, incarcerated in the state to be tamed, and discover bad conscience so that they can hurt themselves, after the more natural outlet of this wish to hurt had been blocked.

# 5 The Individual

> Over the course of its development, the capitalist system has been defended according to a set of assumptions, principles and theories based on the perceived interests of the individual. . . . The tendency to posit the centrality of the individual has been continuous throughout the history of modern capitalism accumulation.
>
> Michael O'Flynn (2009:1), *Profitable Ideas: The Ideology of the Individual in Capitalist Development* (© Michael O'Flynn. Republished with permission of Brill Publishers, permission conveyed through Copyright Clearance Center, Inc.)

In Chapter 2 *Gods*, we saw that seventeenth-century philosopher John Locke (1690[1980]) constructed the early intellectual foundations of liberalism: linking together a conceptualisation of individual sovereignty, the commoditisation of labour and the propertied individual's rights of ownership over such. In arguing for the centrality of sovereign individuality, Locke can be understood as drawing upon his original Calvinist roots. Calvinists had separated from the Catholic Church in the sixteenth century, protesting the Church's mediation between a worshipper and God. Weber (1930[2001]), as we saw, had identified Calvinism as instrumental in the construction of an isolated, personally responsible individuality in religious matters. Such a conceptualisation for Weber ushered in the kind of individualised moral subjectivity necessary for the birth of Capitalism. Considering this period of history in the West, Marcuse (1941[2005]:139) observed,

> If we try to assemble in one guiding concept the various religious, political and economic tendencies which shaped the idea of the individual in the sixteenth and seventeenth century, we may define the individual as the subject of certain fundamental standards and values which no external authority was supposed to encroach upon.

Of course, the category of the individual is not constructed once and for all by Locke and his contemporaries. It was to be drawn in more detail by writers, philosophers, scholars of jurisprudence and others throughout later periods. A century after Locke was writing, the French Revolution would mark a major point of punctuation in the development of the category of the liberal individual. The first major legislative product of the Revolution, the 1789 'Declaration of the Rights of Man and of the Citizen' (*Déclaration des droits de l'homme et du citoyen*), would enshrine formally universal individual rights. Such universalism was contested, however, even at the time. Olympe De Georges (1791) would pen the 'Declaration of the Rights of Woman and the Female Citizen' (*Déclaration des droits de la femme et de la citoyenne*) to object—at the cost of her own life—to the Declaration's subsummation of the sovereignty of women. In relation to all persons, though, the Declaration and the broader Revolution were far from universal in their implications and effects. Setting the scene for most scholarship on the event over the next century, Marx would argue that the French Revolution was a bourgeois revolution: 'the heroes as well as the parties and the masses of the old French Revolution, performed the task of their time—that of unchaining and establishing modern bourgeois society' (Marx 1852:5). As with Locke's writings a century before, it was the sovereignty and autonomy of the independently wealthy, propertied individual that was privileged in the Revolution's Declaration. The propertied individual must, in relation to his own property, have 'the powers of a king to use or abuse at his discretion', as Diderot would aver (Laski 1936:216–217).

The explicit intersection of individual liberty and property was legislated in Article II of the Declaration: 'The aim of every political association is the protection of the natural and imprescriptible rights of man; these rights are liberty, property, security and resistance to oppression'. We can see such privileging of the sovereignty of the propertied individual too in the writings of prominent French and British thinkers of the period. Voltaire in *Dictionnaire Philosophique*, for example, would argue that it is 'inevitable that mankind should be divided into two classes with many sub-divisions—the oppressors and the oppressed. Fortunately, use and wont and the lack of leisure prevent most of the oppressed from realizing their condition' (cited in Laski 1936:222). Similarly, in *Siècle de Louise XIV*, he would argue that the 'labourer and the artisan must be cut down to necessaries, if they are to work: this is human nature. It is inevitable that the majority should be poor; it is only not necessary that it should be wretched' (ibid). The unnecessary state of wretchedness, however, was apparently not to preclude enforced ignorance. Voltaire was to congratulate the jurist La Chalotais in prohibiting educational studies to the working man (Voltaire's letters of February 28, 1763, cited in Laski 1936[2014]) and argue, in a letter to Damilaville (on April 1, 1766, ibid), that as anyone who owned property and needed servants would agree, maintaining the masses in a state of uneducated ignorance was essential. Such views were far from Voltaire's alone. Linguet, for example, would write that 'The condition of society condemns him [the working man] to the use of his physical strength alone. Everything would be lost once he knew that he had a mind' (ibid:220).

The privileging of the interests of individuals with property over those without was replicated across the English Channel. 'Everyone but an idiot knows that the lower classes must be kept poor, or they will never be industrious', Arthur Young would write in 1771 (Young 1771:361, ibid:207). For Patrick Colquhoun, there could be no wealth without

> a large proportion of poverty . . . riches are the offspring of labour, while labour can result only from a state of poverty. . . . Poverty, therefore, is a most necessary and indispensable ingredient in society, without which nations and communities could not exist in a state of civilization.
>
> (Colquhoun 1806:7, ibid:208)

Others' poverty could be dangerous, however, to the man of property. Thus, Adam Smith would write that the protection of property was the chief function of justice.

> The affluence of the rich excites the indignation of the poor, who are often driven by want and prompted by envy to invade their possessions. It is only under the shelter of the civil magistrate that the owner of that valuable property, acquired by the labour of many years, or perhaps many successive generations, can sleep a single night in security.
>
> (Smith 1776, Book V: 1, ii, ibid:198)

Notwithstanding that the strong arm of the law was ever required to enforce it, the blatantly injurious *laissez-faire* labour market was assigned the status of a natural and God-given economic law. Edmund Burke, for example, would regard any attempts by the state or legislator to interfere in the price offered to labour as disastrous, unnatural and a violation of the rights of the employer. And the employer's rights were naturally so much greater than employees'. Like his contemporaries, Burke would have no hesitation in assigning full liberty and political rights only to the propertied, such was the 'inarticulate major premise' of all of his work (ibid:199).

The prejudices of classical liberalism would be revived in more contemporary times. The category of the individual would figure as a central mobilising resource within neoliberalism and would become 'one of the constitutive doctrines of modern society' (Meyer 1986:208). As Harvey (2005:5) writes,

> The founding figures of neoliberal thought took political ideals of human dignity and individual freedom as fundamental, as 'the central

values of civilization'. In so doing they chose wisely, for these are indeed compelling and seductive ideals. These values, they held, were threatened not only by fascism, dictatorships, and communism, but by all forms of state intervention that substituted collective judgements for those of individuals free to choose.

Hayek, for example, would structure his grand neoliberal tract, *The Constitution of Liberty* (1960), around the concept of individual liberty. Defining liberty in classic liberal negative terms as 'independence of the arbitrary will of another' (ibid:12), Hayek uses the concept to construct a number of arguments which though familiar to those living under neoliberal conditions are still nauseating when written as explicit positions. Inequality, for example, is a clear social good:

> some must lead, and the rest must follow . . . the rich, by experimenting with new styles of living not yet accessible to the poor, perform a necessary service without which the advance of the poor would be very much slower.
>
> (p. 41)

Apparently, this holds too for international inequality, where 'the prospect of the poorer "underdeveloped" countries reaching the present level of the West is very much better than it would have been, had the West not pulled so far ahead' (p. 42). While within the nation state, independently wealthy individuals are understood as fundamental for advancing cultural life.

> The leadership of individuals or groups who can back their beliefs financially is particularly essential in the field of cultural amenities, in the fine arts, in education and research, in the preservation of natural beauty and historical treasures, and, above all, in the propagation of new ideas in politics, morals, and religion.
>
> (p. 109)

And

> However important the independent owner of property may be for the economic order of a free society, his importance is perhaps even greater in the field of thought and opinion, of tastes and beliefs. There is something seriously lacking in a society in which all the intellectual, moral, and artistic leaders belong to the employed class.
>
> (p. 111)

Such essential service which the 'private owner of substantial property' (p. 109) performs is replicated within work organisations. The freedom of the masses to sell their labour—which is 'the preferred position of the majority of the population' (p. 107)—means that they can enjoy an existence untroubled by the 'responsibilities of those who control resources and who must concern themselves constantly with new arrangements and combinations' (p. 106). These 'independent individuals who can take the initiative in the continuous process of re-forming and redirecting organizations' are thus understood to generate the 'multiplicity of opportunities for employment' for the masses (p. 108). As such, naturally, the rewards and remuneration that accrue to these 'men who act on their own initiative' must not be measured 'according to what others think he deserves' or on the basis of what is 'generally regarded as just' by those who, being mere employees of larger organisations, are 'relieved of some of the responsibilities of economic life' (p. 107). Even in those larger organisations, Hayek's blatantly normative privileging of independently wealthy individuals as the driving force and central moral subject of 'progressive' society pertains. We are told that it is the actions of propertied individuals at the top that really matter, as 'the outstanding success even of large and well-established corporations is often due to some single person who has achieved his position of independence and influence through control of large means' (p. 108).

Of course, outside of the texts of liberal and neoliberal ideologues, a discourse of individual liberty has long been deployed in the management of the labour process. For example, employers' evidence to the House of Commons, reported in 1751, decried any attempt to regulate the price paid for labour as 'at the very least inequitable', doing an injurious disservice to the diverse capacities of individual workmen (cited in Laski 1936:176); in the 1840s employers denounced restrictions on the length of the working day as 'ruthlessly sacrific[ing] the unfortunate factory workers to [a] mania for improving the world' (cited in Marx 1867[1990]:396–397); at the start of the twentieth century, F. W. Taylor (1911) provided almost utopian descriptions of the benefits for the liberty of individual workmen who followed the prescriptions of Scientific Management; assaults on trade unions throughout the 1980s and 'flexibility' in the conditions proffered by the employer became 'part of the neoliberal rhetoric that could be persuasive to individual labourers, particularly those who had been excluded from the monopoly benefits that strong unionization sometimes conferred' (Harvey 2005:53); and 'neo-totalitarian' (Willmott 1993) corporate cultures were cast as arenas that 'give people control over their destinies' and that 'let, even insist, that people stick out' (Peters and Waterman 1982:238–239).

O'Flynn (2009:1) perhaps sums up this section well with his observation that '(t)he desire to maximize individual freedom and the desire to minimize obstacles to capital accumulation have long been expressed in the same breath. This has been very useful with regard to the legitimization of the system as a whole'.

## Critics of the Individual

The undoubted usefulness of the category of the individual, and the ideal of individual liberty, to legitimise capitalism has not prevented it from generating extensive criticism. Critics of the idea of the individual go back a long way and come from various genres. We saw in Chapter 3 that early modern writers such as Marlowe and Milton would characterise the desire for individual sovereignty amongst early and emerging capitalists as an irreligious even satanic drive to go beyond natural and God-given limits on the powers one should aspire to in a lifetime. Later writers would critique the nature of individuality that was proffered further—and would do so even at the high point of liberalism, Victorian society. 'The wretchedness, desire, repression, punitive discipline and spiritual hunger which mark the Brontës' fiction', for example, 'intensely personal though they are, also speak of a whole society in traumatic transition' (Eagleton 2005:127). Irreducible and sovereign individuals are not the substance of such works, rather, as with Charlotte Brontë's heroines, they are 'divided selves',

> women who are outwardly demure yet inwardly passionate, full of erotic and imaginative hungering which must be locked back upon itself in meekness, self-sacrifice and stoic endurance . . . it speaks eloquently of the situation of all women of intellect and aspiration in a stifling patriarchal order.
>
> (ibid:129–130)

In the novels of Thomas Hardy, characters 'live out a conflict between the way they experience themselves as living subjects, and the way they appear in the objectifying gaze of others'; they are driven to a 'schizoid solution to the conflict, splitting yourself in two and contemplating yourself as though you were someone else' (Eagleton 2005:194 and 196). Jude Fawley, for example, the central character of *Jude the Obscure*, 'wandering through Christminster as a shabby, anonymous workman, begins to feel like a ghost. If enough passers-by stare through you, you feel absent to yourself. This is a society which uses your body, but which disembodies you in the process' (ibid:195). Hardy's novel shows that liberalism's purely negative conceptualisation of individual freedom

> is at once vitally necessary and ultimately insufficient, compared to that corporate or collective freedom which Jude himself advocates, and which is the ethic of the emergent labour movement. In this sense, *Jude* explores the limits of liberalism. It exposes the lie of freedom of choice in an oppressive society, without abandoning what is precious in that creed.
>
> (ibid:211)

The 'ardent, tireless reformer' (ibid:162), Charles Dickens, would produce works which denounced the squalor and destitution that was the consequence of a *laissez-faire* economy. His industrially set novel *Hard Times*, for example,

> manifests its identity as a polemical work, a critique of mid-Victorian industrial society dominated by materialism, acquisitiveness, and ruthlessly competitive capitalist economics. . . . He repudiates the employers' exploitation of their power . . . their reliance on *laissez fair* . . . their withdrawal from social contract with the working classes . . . their mental habit of regarding the workers as soulless units in the economic machine.
>
> (Lodge 1966:145)

Of course, the writings which, more than any others, presented a radical critique of liberal Victorian society and its ideal of sovereign individuality were those of Karl Marx. In *Volume One* of *Capital* (1867[1990]), for example, Marx would draw upon parliamentary reports and journalism of the time to document what the liberty accorded the propertied buyer of labour meant for the individual workman, woman and child. In the Nottingham lace trade, for example,

> Children of nine or ten years are dragged from their squalid beds at two, three, or four o'clock in the morning and compelled to work for a bare subsistence until ten, eleven, or twelve at night, their limbs wearing away, their frames dwindling, their faces whitening, and their humanity absolutely sinking into a stone-like torpor, utterly horrible to contemplate. . . . The system, as Rev. Montagu Valpy describes it, is one of unmitigated slavery, socially, physically, morally, and spiritually. . . . What can be thought of a town which holds a public meeting to petition that the period of labour for men shall be diminished to eighteen hours a day?
>
> (*The Daily Telegraph*, 17th January 1860 in Marx 1867:353)

In the pottery districts of Staffordshire, children as young as 7 worked 15 hours a day (*Children's Employment Commission, First Report*, 1863, ibid:354), average life expectancy was 'extraordinarily low', and the hours and conditions of labour were such that each 'successive generation of potters is more dwarfed and less robust than the preceding one' (*Public Health, Third Report*, ibid:354–355). And in workplaces as varied as dressmaking establishments, matchstick manufacturers and the blacksmith's forge, people were quite literally worked to death (ibid:364–366). As Marx would observe, in

> its insatiable appetite for surplus labour, capital oversteps not only the moral but even the merely physical limits of the working day. It

usurps the time for growth, development and healthy maintenance of the body. It steals the time required for the consumption of fresh air and sunlight. . . . It extends the worker's production-time within a given period by shortening his life.

(ibid:375–377)

Informing his exposure of the conditions of labour was Marx's critical reconceptualisation of the individual under liberalism. Far from being a unified, sovereign entity, Marx would present the individual as radically alienated and estranged: divided from themselves, their labour, their species and nature (Marx 1844a). In developing these ideas, Marx was drawing heavily upon Feuerbach's critique of religion as self-alienation. 'God', Feuerbach (1890:32) would argue, 'is the highest subjectivity of man abstracted from himself; hence man can do nothing of himself, all goodness comes from God. The more subjective God is, the more completely does man divest himself of his subjectivity'. Religion represented

the disuniting of man from himself . . . in religion man contemplates his own latent nature. Hence it must be shown that this antithesis, this differencing of God and man, with which religion begins, is a differencing of man with his own nature.

(Feuerbach 1890:34)

Marx's important contribution was in extending this critique of religious alienation to the economic realm and the material circumstances that individuals found themselves under conditions of liberal capitalism. 'It is the immediate task of philosophy', he would write,

to unmask self-estrangement in its unholy forms once the holy form of human self-estrangement has been unmasked. Thus the criticism of heaven turns into the criticism of earth, the criticism of religion into the criticism of law and the criticism of theology into the criticism of politics.

(Marx 1844b[1992]:244–245)

Critics of work and organisation throughout the nineteenth and twentieth centuries would draw upon ideas of alienation and estrangement to read the individual as multiply divided and degraded in relation to their own labour and work organisations. Through the organisation of the labour process, individuals had lost the 'human unity of hand and brain', such that these had become 'divided and hostile' (Braverman 1974:125). They had become estranged from their own emotions and authentic sense of self through the deep acting required of the service worker (Hochschild 1983) and the dramaturgical commitment of the corporately cultured (Kunda 2006). They had been divided from awareness of individual ethical responsibility through role identification and the distancing effects of bureaucracy and hierarchy (Arendt 1963; Bauman 1989; Jackall 1988). They had lost their character (Sennet 1998) and had become separated from community (Putnam 2000) through the demands of an enterprise culture and greedy workplaces (Coser 1974). The size and scale of corporate structures had divided them from any sense of individual purpose or power (Mills 1951), and discourses of business leadership had further alienated organisational members, emotionally and intellectually deskilling them on a societal-wide scale (Gemmil and Oakley 1992). Ultimately, 'advanced industrial civilization' had resulted in 'the suppression of individuality in the mechanization of socially necessary but painful performances' (Marcuse 1964[2002]:3). Taking these points together,

> the individualist order of the modern Western world has met with challenges that have rendered its beliefs and doctrines problematic. Historical developments in the material and social realms, such as industrialization and the emergence of mass society, have altered the ontological foundations of individual identity.
>
> (Heller and Wellbery 1986:1)

The result being that

> the traditional view of the fully integrated, unique, and distinctive person has been severely compromised by a variety of factors, commonly accepted as causing the fragmentation of self and the perceived decline in the belief that the 'individual' is a legitimate social reality.
>
> (Brilliant 1991:171)

Such ontological challenge to individuality was paralleled by strong philosophical contestation that both built upon and diverged from Marx's earlier critique. Feminist, postcolonial, queer, psychoanalytic, poststructuralist and other works read the sovereign individual as a fiction or ideological device. Freudian psychoanalysis, for example, would radically undermine 'notions about autonomy, individual choice, will, responsibility, and rationality, showing that we do not control our own lives in the most fundamental sense' and would make it impossible 'to think about the self in any simple way, to talk blithely about the individual' (Chodorow 1986:197). Meanwhile, structuralist and post-structuralist works would negate 'the normative power of autonomous individuality by reducing subjective consciousness to the artefact of a self-replicating, superpersonal mechanism' (Heller and Wellbery 1986:7). Taken together, the conditions experienced by, and criticisms of, the liberal individual expressed in this section attest to Greenblatt's (1986:33) observation that

> [e]ven though we still inhabit a moral and psychological system based upon our legitimate existence as individuals, that existence has come

to seem strange—as if the very basis of our idea of nature were itself revealed to be a cunningly wrought artifice.

## Critics for the Individual

Notwithstanding its co-option within neo/liberalism and critique at the hands of post/structuralisms, 'some form of individualism', as Heller and Wellbery (1986:1) observe, 'has been a key factor in the life of the West for the last five hundred years'. Reflecting upon the above sections, we could be forgiven for coming to the conclusion that this long-gestating category of the individual is irredeemably uncritical—that the category should be dispensed with, perhaps to be replaced with 'the subject' understood in its structuralist and post-structuralist guise as being subject to power and to the Other. Jettisoning the category of the individual would however, I think, be premature—not least because to do so would be to accede to neo/liberalism a category that still has much seductive appeal (Harvey 2005) and about which we may have forgotten its history and import (Siedentop 2014).

   Some of the import of the individual can be gleaned from the writings of Critical Theory, in particular the linking of the category of the individual to the exercise of critical reason, to freedom of the will and, thereby, even to the possibility of ethics. Horkheimer, in *The End of Reason*, would argue that the central moral philosophical concept of Critical Theory—if not Western philosophy more generally—was critical reason.

> The fundamental concepts of civilization are in the process of rapid decay. . . . The question of how far these concepts are at all valid clamors more than ever for answer. The decisive concept among them was that of reason, and philosophy knew of no higher principle.
>
> (Horkheimer 1941:27)

Much of the work of Critical Theorists would focus upon the capture of reason in modern society. As Marcuse, for example, would argue in his 1941 essay *Some Social Implications of Modern Technology*, liberal society was founded upon the ideal of the human individual

> as the subject of certain fundamental standards and values which no external authority was supposed to encroach upon. These standards and values pertained to the forms of life, social as well as personal, which were most adequate to the full development of man's faculties and abilities.
>
> (pp. 139–140)

As a rational being, the individual

> was deemed capable of finding these forms by his own thinking and, once he had acquired freedom of thought, of pursuing the course of

action which would actualize them. Society's task was to grant him such freedom and to remove all restrictions upon his rational course of action.

(ibid:140)

Free competition was enshrined as the basis upon which such individuals could best pursue their own interests. However, competition led to consolidation of property and an imperative to grasp the competitive benefits of machine production and mechanistic organisation. As a result, there was a progressive eradication of the 'costs' of non-productive, non-instrumental or non-machine-like behaviour and attitudes. This was accompanied and preceded by a subordination of reason—first of the owner of production, then the employee and eventually all citizens—to the logic of machine production, the structures of mechanistic large-scale organisations, to a technological rationality. As large-scale mass production and mechanistic organisations dominated the landscape, what seemed reasonable was for individuals to work out how best to survive in the face of apparently overwhelming structures, 'through reason the individual asserts or adapts himself and gets along in society. It induces the individual to subordinate himself to society whenever he is not powerful enough to pattern society upon his own interests' (Horkheimer 1941:28–29). 'He is rational who most efficiently accepts and executes what is allocated to him, who entrusts his fate to the large scale enterprises and organizations which administer the apparatus' (Marcuse 1941:157).

The nature of reason embodied by advanced capitalist society, however, was only a faint shadow of what was once hoped for it. This more profound conceptualisation of reason would link reason with morality, it would be 'a mode of thought and action which is geared to reduce ignorance, destruction, brutality, and oppression' (Marcuse 1964:145). What was rational was that which furthered human and other life; what was irrational was that which harmed or cheapened that life. Reason in this understanding had a 'subversive power', the power to subject the 'facts', or what seems oppressively inevitable, to a higher set of ideals. If the present was found wanting, then we could work towards changing the present, and thereby seek to establish 'the truth for men and things—that is, the conditions in which men and things become what they really are' (ibid:127). Reason in this sense was far more than what it risked becoming—a narrow means–ends rationality or an accommodation to a brutal or overbearing corporatised world. Reason was unashamedly utopian, imaginative, idealistic. As such it represented both the unique nature of humankind and the way to realise that nature by creating a society that accommodated it.

In holding to this broader conceptualisation of reason, Critical Theorists were joined to a far longer lineage of moral philosophy. This would include both Weber and Marx. Weber's distinction between different rationalities—*Zweckrational* or instrumental rationality and the

*Wertrational* or substantive rationality—and his critique of the increasing disenchantment of society, its reduction to instrumental rationality, privileging of calculation over substance, bureaucratisation and mechanisation, all figure strongly. Marx, whose formative influence on Critical Theory is well established, conceived of humankind as having a particular species-nature founded upon the way that we execute our labour in the world: that is, our unique potential to conceive of something in imagination before we execute it in reality (Marx 1867). Building on this was the idea that people can transform or revolutionise both the physical and the social world so as to eradicate the imperative to exploit others for individual gain: thereby to make a world that more readily conforms to the conditions and relations that foster human fulfilment. In his focus on the transformation of the real world towards a more rational ideal, Marx was to make an important break from his teacher Hegel as well as Hegelians such as Feuerbach. Where Hegel would see an idealised and abstracted logic or spirit working its way through world events, Marx would emphasise the progressive material transformation of the world as a direct result of human agency (Marx 1843). Reason then for Marx, including our longing for an ideal and less oppressive future, was not just abstract or philosophical speculation (Marx 1845). Rather reason was normative *and* materialist. We projected ourselves out of the present and direct ourselves to make that projected future a reality. In Marcuse's (1964:145) words, 'Reason becomes historical Reason'.

While Critical Theory's conceptualisation of reason would owe much to Weber and Marx, the larger debt was to the subject of Horkheimer's post-doctoral thesis: Immanuel Kant. Kant made the crucial distinction between reason and understanding. Understanding was cognition of experience, the knowledge of how things currently are. Such understanding was necessary and valuable, of course. But it was only a kind of accounting or tabulation of the present. Reason thus understood 'declares its right to make demands upon experience in a manner forbidden to understanding' (Neiman 1994:5). Reason was the capacity to determine ends—and to subject experience to these ends. And this was irreducibly individual. No one, in Kant's system of philosophy, not scholars or politicians, not the propertied, not moral philosophers, had a privileged claim to deduce what ought to be. In the Kantian refusal to countenance the subordination of individual reason, we can see the philosophical roots of Critical Theory's opposition to an orthodox Marxist position that reduced people to mere bearers of social classes, their economic location—or indeed to being only 'subject to'. Though they were acutely aware of the totalitarian assault on individual liberty and the totalising effects of massive organisations, mass production and mass culture, Kantian philosophical roots enabled Critical Theory to retain a central and abiding interest in the category of the individual and the transformative ethical potential of individual thought and reason.

## The Individual's Religious Birth

While Critical Theorists would chart conceptual linkage to Kant's writings on the individual, ethics and reason, such ideas can be traced rather further back—specifically to the break that Christian theology and practices made from the Roman world. In the previous chapter we saw how Foucault (2005) would highlight Christian confessional and spiritual practices as 'an absolutely crucial moment in the history of subjectivity in the West . . . when the task and obligation of truth-telling about oneself is inserted within the procedure indispensable for salvation' (p. 364). Such a formula, for Foucault, 'did not exist at all in Greek, Hellenistic, or Roman Antiquity' (ibid). Arendt, in the *Life of the Mind* (1971b), would take us back to the same historical moment in her examination of the foundations of individual critical thought. Examining the roots of the idea of free will, an idea which serves as the 'necessary postulate of every ethics and every system of laws' in modernity (1971b, Volume 2:5), Arendt would argue that 'the faculty of the Will was unknown to Greek antiquity and was discovered as a result of experiences about which we hear next to nothing before the first century of the Christian era' (ibid:3). As Kristeva (2001:202) would observe in discussing this work, 'Arendt deciphered the key moments in Christian theology that construe thinking as life or as a life of the mind'. In more recent work, Agamben (2011) too has considered the formative legacy that early Christian theology provided in constructing modernity's notion of free will and ethics.

> Ethics in a modern sense, with its court of insoluble aporias, is born . . . from the fracture between being and praxis that is produced at the end of the ancient world and has its eminent place in Christian theology. If the notion of free will, which is, all things considered, marginal in classical thought, becomes the central category first of Christian theology and then of the ethics and ontology of modernity, this happens because these find in the above-mentioned fracture their original site and will have to confront it right to the end.
>
> (ibid:54)

As Agamben argued, the concept of God's divine free will which is central to Christianity marked a radical ontological rupture from the classical tradition: 'what is new is the division between being and the will, nature and action, introduced by Christian theology' (p. 55). The God of Christianity creates the world as an act of will, not because s/he is compelled to or because it is her/his nature to do so. The

> very motif of creation ex nihilo emphasizes the autonomy and freedom of divine praxis. God has not created the world due to a necessity of his nature or his being, but because he wanted it. To the question

'why did God make heaven and earth?' Augustine answers: 'quia voluit', 'because he wished to'.

(p. 56)

God and, later, Jesus are anarchic—uncaused and undetermined (p. 56).

If we do not understand this original 'anarchic' vocation of Christology, it is not even possible to understand the subsequent historical development of Christian theology, with its latent atheological tendency, or the history of Western philosophy, with its ethical caesura between ontology and praxis . . . what is at stake between these two is the idea of freedom.

(pp. 58–59)

It is, as Agamben states, not merely God that is constructed in Christianity. Through centuries of theological doctrine and related religio-cultural practices, free will—which is understood as the nature of the Christian God—is stitched into the category of the individual, a category which comes to define the citizenry of the West. Just how significant a departure from classical ontology this construction of the individual was, how 'utterly remote' (p. 9) the morality of the classical world would be to us, has been examined in Siedentop's (2014) *Inventing the Individual: The Origins of Western Liberalism*. Siedentop reveals how in the ancient world the family, not the individual, was the basic and defining unit of social reality. The ancient paterfamilias 'was a veritable church. It was a church which constrained its members to an extent that can scarcely be exaggerated. The father, representing all his ancestors, was himself a god in preparation' (p. 15). Worship at the sacred fire, the family hearth, defined the beliefs and behaviours of family members. The authority of the father 'as priest and magistrate' was absolute. It represented 'the overwhelming imperative to preserve the family worship, and so to prevent the ancestors, untended, being cast into oblivion' (p. 15). Property rights strictly followed this absolute privileging of the family, 'property belonged not to an individual man, but to the family . . . the Greeks and Romans understood property primarily as a means of perpetuating the family worship' (p. 16). Plato, for instance, would be contemptuous of a dying man's wish to dispose of his property,

Thou who are only a pilgrim here below, does it belong to thee to decide such affairs? Thou art the master neither of thy property nor of thyself; thou and thy estate, all these things, belong to thy family; that is to say, to thy ancestors and to thy posterity.

(*Laws*, cited in Siedentop 2014:17)

As populations grow and consolidate, federations of paterfamilias consolidate into the ancient city. However, piety to the paterfamilias is retained and full citizen status of the city is frequently reserved only for the father of the family. 'The city that emerged was thus a confederation of cults, an association superimposed on other associations, all modelled on the family and its worship. The ancient city was not an association of individuals' (p. 21). The family/city was everything: morality, religion, identity.

> The successive worships into which the ancient citizen was initiated left no space for individual conscience or choice. These worships claimed authority over not just his actions but also his thoughts. Their rules governed his relations with himself as well as others. There was no sphere of life into which these rules could not enter.
>
> (p. 22)

Modelled upon the family, its ancestors and the authority of the father, an assumption of immutable natural inequality defined the ancient world—and with this certain other values, including profound contempt for labour and those that laboured, and an admiration for military valour, representing the protection of the city/family (p. 36).

Roman conquest and distant imperial rule starkly demonstrated a new fragility of the paterfamilias' authority—and other religious beliefs gained ground and influence amongst subjugated populations. Jewish beliefs in particular garnered much interest, 'the image of a single, remote and inscrutable God dispensing his laws to a whole people corresponded to the experience of peoples who were being subjugated to the Roman *imperium*' (p. 53). As Roman conquest extends further, Judaism becomes more volatile and fractured, giving rise to a number of Messianic and apocalyptic movements: one of which would be the Jesus movement. The account that arose amongst the followers of this movement—of the death and resurrection of Jesus—provided the idea of the individual with perhaps its first truly significant moment.

> First, Jesus crucified; then, Jesus resurrected. Previously in antiquity, it was the patriarchal family that had been the agency of immortality. Now, through the story of Jesus, individual moral agency was raised up as providing a unique window into the nature of things, into the experience of grace rather than necessity, a glimpse of something transcending death.
>
> (p. 58)

The writings of Saul of Tarsus, canonised as St Paul, were the earliest surviving writings of the Jesus movement. Paul's formulation of Jesus' teachings presented a theology which would become crucial in the unfolding construction of the individual. In Paul's works we have the beginnings of ideas of human equality rather than natural inequality. 'There is neither Jew nor Greek, there is neither slave nor free, there is neither male nor female; for you are all one in Christ Jesus' (Galatians 3:28). Social roles and class distinctions still existed, of course, but they were not as hitherto to be all defining. All could experience and express the new morality of God's love through their own acts as individuals. Paul's writing 'provided an ontological foundation for the "individual", through the promise that humans have access to the deepest reality as individuals rather than merely as members of a group' (Siendetop 2014:63), though that individuality itself would now be premised upon submission 'to the mind and will of God as revealed in the Christ' (p. 65). The idea of inner depth, of looking within to see the presence of Christ in your soul, marked the beginning of the process of self-questioning, which we see enacted in such an influential manner in Augustine's later confessions, giving birth to what was possibly the originary hermeneutics of the self. The Pauline construction of Jesus' message 'had fostered the sense of a realm of conscience that demanded respect. Individual agency and divine agency were now understood as parts of a continuum' (p. 68).

The Pauline theological introduction of individual will and conscience would take centuries of reinterpretation and uneven translation to transform the social practices and relations of the West. By the third century, for example, when Christianity had already assumed a significant presence in Roman society, the periodic execution of Christian martyrs was formative in underlining a moral archetype quite distinct from the classical ideal of the martially adept hero. In making martyrs of Christians,

> the ancient world was consecrating what it sought to destroy and destroying what it sought to preserve. For the Christian martyrs gained a hold over the popular imagination. . . . The martyrs offered a model of heroism open to all. . . . As Tertullian remarked early in the third century, the martyrs blood provided 'the seed of the church'.
>
> (p. 80)

Such openness was reflected in the practices of the Christian churches. Both the wealthy and the poor, women and men, 'approached the sacraments of the church. They were baptised and received the Eucharist as individuals seeking salvation, rather than as members of a group' (p. 83). Christian groups that did form, notably the early monasteries—and later convents—which drew together the solitary faithful who had chosen to live outside of city and family, represented a new form of community, one based upon 'voluntary association, in individual acts of will' (p. 94); this was a 'sociability founded on the role of individual conscience' (p. 95). The foundation of ascetic communities of women marked an unprecedented cleaving of women from permanent subordination to the family and to sexual subordination (p. 95). The early monasteries were important in connecting other values and practices too with the idea of living a Christian life. Work—labour—for instance, which had been an object of profound disdain in the ancient world, was rehabilitated and acquired 'a new dignity, becoming even a requirement of self-respect' (p. 95). Rule in the monasteries too departed from the ancient aristocratic structures and demonstrated formative attempts to democratise authority. Basil of Caesarea, an influential theologian of the fourth century, would stress the importance of compassionate efforts and exchanges—both between the monastic community and the outside world and also between the superiors of the monastery and the monks under their charge.

> This one thing, then, is essential in the superior . . . he must be compassionate, showing long-suffering to those who through inexperience fall short in their duty, not passing sins over in silence but meekly bearing with the restive, applying remedies to them all with kindness.
> (Basil of Caesarea, quoted in Dunn 2003, cited in Siedentop 2014:97)

Similarly, the Rule of St Benedict in the sixth century, influential in the structuring of the monasteries in subsequent centuries, 'sought to eliminate social distinctions within the monastery', to temper monastic government with a 'listening culture', and to 'respect the different needs of individual monks' (p. 97). The struggle for self-control and self-rule, which had defined monks from the beginning in their solitary retreats from familial and city life, developed into a 'stringent but self-imposed' obedience to monastic rules.

> Monasticism consecrated a vision of social order found on conscience, on hard won individual intentions rather than publically enforced status differences. . . . Liberty, it now seemed, consisted in obedience to rules that an individual's conscience imposed on itself.
>
> (p. 98)

Outside of the monastic communities, such ideas would take longer to bite into the practices of the still largely aristocratically organised wider society—though even here they eventually would do so. In the eighth century, for example, Charlemagne—King of the Franks and Holy Roman Emperor—asked for oaths of allegiance from every person in his realm. The oath, to serve Charlemagne 'with all my will and with what understanding God has given me' (cited in Siendentop 2014:153), was to be sworn by freemen, by women and even by slaves on royal lands. What was striking about such a practice was the assumption that all persons, including even those in servitude, had innerness, an individual conscience and will, which it was necessary for the ruler to acknowledge and to seek the loyalty of. Over the centuries that followed, the idea of the individual, which began with the Pauline translation of the message of the Jesus movement, would continue to make advances into the fabric and identity of the West—culminating, as we observed in earlier sections of this chapter, with its co-option by neo/liberalism, its critique at the hands of various post/structuralist traditions and its identification by Critical Theorists as the essential but threatened foundation of critical reason and, ultimately, ethics.

## Ethics, Others and the Plural Individual

Remembering that the individual is not merely an ideological construction of neo/liberalism, that it may in fact be understood as a complex product of two millennia's gestation and translation, might well suggest the category for renewed examination by critical scholars of organisation. And one of the things that a renewed examination may offer, I suggest, is a reconceptualisation of ethical subjectivity. I have argued previously (Wray-Bliss 2002, 2009, 2016) that while critical organisational scholarship examines and theorises the political within work and labour relations very well—the rich traditions of Labour Process Theory, Industrial Relations and Critical Management Studies are testament to this—it has shown a reticence to similarly engage with the ethical. With notable exceptions (see Rhodes and Wray-Bliss 2013 for a review), scholars have either shied away from ethics, have treated it as a managerialist ploy to disguise processes of exploitation and accumulation, or have reduced ethics to a political device—the means by which power enters into the subjectivities of the governed. Relatively few works have explored ethics in terms of the actions and choices of individual subjects of organisation (e.g. Watson 2003; Collins and Wray-Bliss 2005; McMurray, Pullen and Rhodes 2011): those acts of individual will and unpredictable conscience which we may increasingly need to look to and understand in contexts defined by isomorphic pressures towards conformity and instrumental rationality (Arendt 1963; Bauman 1989; Marcuse 1941, 1964).

Part of the reticence and relative neglect of ethics by critical organisational scholars would seem to stem from the concern that discussion of ethics necessarily reproduce ideas of voluntarism, autonomy and ethical sovereignty, leaving us with 'nothing to argue about other than each other's value preferences' (Thompson, Smith and Ackroyd 2000:1156). A number of scholars have drawn upon the work of philosopher Emmanuel Levinas to conceptualise ethics in ways that resist such problems (e.g. Byers and Rhodes 2007; Jones 2007; Jones, Parker and ten Bos 2005; Kaulingfreks and ten Bos 2007; Soares 2003; Roberts 2001; Weiskopf and Willmott 2013; Wray-Bliss 2013). For Levinas, the self is not the origin of ethics. Ethics does not originate with the person who, from a position of independence and distance, voluntarily thinks themselves into relations of responsibility to others. Ethics originates from without, in the form of another person. This other is radically not reducible to oneself. They are Other: alterity. Their existence voices a silent but constant call on our responsibility. They fundamentally destabilise a belief in one's primacy. 'We name this calling into question of my spontaneity by the present of the Other ethics' (ibid 1969:43). For Levinas then, to be ethical is no longer to be understood as vested in a position of sovereign and autonomous individuality. It is not an individual who chooses to be ethical. This new ethics is instead the 'subjectivity of the hostage' (Derrida 1991:112, also Levinas 1998:11), hostage to an unending demand of responsibility to the Other, a demand which compels ethical response from the self. By positioning the other rather than the self as the origins of ethics, this conceptualisation seeks to elide problems of sovereignty, voluntarism and autonomy which, for Levinas, plague all previous formulations of ethics.

Levinas' conceptualisation of ethics is radical and powerful. However, it is a formulation that contains elements that would seem to make it an unlikely foundation for a wider reengagement with ethics by organisational scholars. First, Levinas represents the call to ethics as akin to violence, a piercing of the sovereignty of the self by an embodied awareness of the vulnerability of the Other. Ethics is exposure to trauma, vulnerability, a nudity more naked than destitution, a skin exposed to wounds, a cheek offered to the smiter (1998:48–49); it is taking 'the bread out of one's own mouth to nourish the hunger of another with one's own fasting' (p. 56); it is 'writhing in the tight dimension of pain' (p. 75); it is even bearing 'responsibility for the persecuting by the persecutor' (p. 75). A conceptualisation of ethics as persecution or mortification of the self does not seem likely to recommend itself to a field of study which seeks to critique the violence, degradations and indignities that people are already subject to in their organised lives (see also Critchley 2007). Second, while Levinas radically challenges the sovereignty of the self as the foundation of ethics, he does so at the risk of instigating a new sovereignty in the form of the Other. The Other is conceptualised as radically different, as alterity, as unknowable and irreducible to our categories of thought, as infinite in the demands that they make upon us. Ethics in Levinas' formulation is not a relationship of mutuality or plurality, something that might undo the binary of self–other. Instead it is a radical privileging of Other over self. The Other as the subject of ethics invades, persecutes, overturns the self. Rather than undoing relations of sovereignty and independence, they are inverted: the Other becomes the independent causal element, the self the caused. Finally, in Levinas' work there is a binary separation of ethics and politics. Ethics is the embodied, sensorial, bodily awareness of responsibility that the proximity of the Other engenders in the self. It is non-rational, non-calculative, non-cognitive and infinite. Politics is a calculative reasoned process by which we seek to make judgements of justice, delineating which ethical responsibility we can hope to realise given resource constraints in the real. As with the binary of self–other, the philosophical dualism of Levinas' conceptualisation of ethics and politics would seem to cut against both movements in organisational scholarship to resist dualistic thinking (Knights 1997), as well as more specific attempts to regard ethics and politics as intimately connected (Parker 1999; Pullen and Rhodes 2015).

Rather than a radical separation of self and other, an ethics understood as violence, and a binary understanding of ethics and politics, is it possible to conceptualise ethics in a way that retains Levinas' remarkable undoing of independence and sovereignty while avoiding the above problematics? Again, reconsideration of the ways that the individual was constructed in formative religious discourse might be useful here. Though the roots of its construction as a social category would, as we have seen above, stretch back at least as far as the Pauline translation of the message of the Jesus movement, the etymological basis of the term 'individual' lie in the early fifteenth century, where it referred to the indivisible nature of the Holy Trinity. This etymological root speaks to a highly significant aspect in the founding construction of the category of the individual, one that may have become lost or obscured in its later liberal, and latterly neoliberal, manifestations. The individual referred, from the outset, not to an atomistic singularity but rather a multiplicity: the trinity, the containment of the Son, the Father and the Holy Spirit in one indivisible entity. The Pauline conceptualisation of the person—later to be called the individual—was similarly non-atomistic and plural. The individual was conceived as a 'mystical union with Christ' (Siedentop 2014:59). 'It is no longer I who live, but Christ who lives in me' (Galatians 2:19–20). By 'creating an inner link between the divine will and human agency', Paul 'conceives the idea that the two can, at least potentially, be fused within each person' (Siedentop 2014:59 and 61). Such fusing was later to be ritualised in the individual receiving the Holy Spirit during baptism and consuming the blood and body of Christ in the Eucharist. By fusing the individual with Christ, the boundaries of ethical regard, which hitherto was restricted to the members of the ancient family/city, was radically broadened. All persons are, in Paul's translation of the Jesus message, God's children ('you are all one in Christ Jesus', Galatians 3:28) and our responsibility is to love all such persons as our new family. This introduced a new moral freedom: freedom from the ancient laws and limits of genealogy, embedded in familial or city rule. However, it was a freedom which came with significant responsibilities,

> you were called to freedom. . . . Only do not use your freedom as an opportunity for the flesh, but through love serve one another. For the whole law is fulfilled in one word. . . . Love your neighbour as yourself.
>
> (Galatians 5:13–14)

Paul's central injunction to love others as yourself offers at least two interpretations. It can be read to mean 'love your neighbour like you love yourself': a reading that is readily available to us, given that it accords with a modern construction of a sovereign and separate individuality and the idea of a narcissistic subject who is being called upon to exercise ethics as an act of charity toward separate others. When we appreciate, though, how the Pauline individual is conceived from the outset as a fusion of non-reducible entities—the self, Christ in the self and the self in Christ—then this can be reinterpreted. It is possible to read Paul's injunction to mean that we love our neighbour because they are, in some way, already part of our self: 'your neighbour *as yourself*'.

James Mensch's (2003) *Ethics and Selfhood* might help us understand the implications of such an idea. Like my reading of your neighbour *as yourself*, Mensch understands the nature of ethics to be vested in the experience of 'oneself as another' (p. 43). By empathising with others, we overlay their experiences and concerns, their views and values, in our own being. Our capacity for empathy is so fundamental to our being that we even feel pain or pleasure in another's experience: we experience joy in their elation, we cry at their loss, we flinch at their being struck. This somatic-empathic process 'is a living *as* another by a living *in* the other. It is a sharing of the other's embodiment. It is "empathy" in the sense of feeling or experiencing in the other's body' (p. 39). 'Empathising and imagining ourselves into their being, these others become part of my self, they are "in" me as other than me' (p. 45). My selfhood 'is a function of the embodiment I imaginatively share in taking up the other's standpoint' (p. 44). I see myself through these others who have taken up home in my imagination and empathy and thus 'I am always being resituated in terms of others' (p. 45). The self then is a kind of plurality. The exercise of empathy 'disrupts self-presence. It makes it dual by including the other' (p. 43), I 'undergo a certain doubling' with these different selves overlaid in my psyche (p. 45). Access to the different viewpoints and experiences of these others in me generates a certain inner distance from the singular demands of my immediate physical self, generating the precious space of freedom required for ethics to surface over compulsion. However, this plurality of others in me presents a challenge of integration, such that

> the primary task of the self is that of managing the dualities of self-presence involved in its being with others. It maintains itself as a functioning self through negotiating the differences involved. Its unity, rather than being taken for granted, is continually at issue in its functioning.
>
> (p. 45)

Ethics in this understanding is neither voluntary nor comes from a place of sovereignty and independence. The freedom to be ethical—the space that is created from immediate ego or physical desires—is engendered by the empathic incorporation of other experiences and viewpoints, by the self's plurality. Ethical choices that a person makes represent for them nothing less than their self-preservation; they are the means by which we negotiate the competing claims within ourselves.

> I must come to terms with the duality of my self-presence that is occasioned by empathy. I have to negotiate the competing claims this makes on me. The ethical system I adopt is, in fact, a set of rules for negotiating these claims. Here, the answer to the question 'Why be ethical?' concerns the selfhood that is the result of such negotiation. Being ethical is its preservation.
>
> (p. 47)

A greater sense of what this might mean can be had if we return briefly to the writings of Hannah Arendt. In *Personal Responsibility under Dictatorship* (1964b), Arendt reflects upon what enables some individuals to resist under conditions of totalitarianism. She describes how the ethical choice not to participate in atrocity did not arise from sophisticated philosophical awareness, it did not stem from the manners of respectable society, nor was it founded upon adherence to long-established social moral norms, norms which proved capable of being inverted with shocking ease. Rather Arendt suggests that those individuals, who without wider support or precedent made the choice not to participate, had simply

> asked themselves to what extent they would still be able to live in peace with themselves after having committed certain deeds; and they decided that it would be better to do nothing, not because the world would then be changed for the better, but simply because only on this condition could they go on living with themselves at all.
>
> (p. 44)

Theirs was a 'disposition to live together explicitly with oneself, to have intercourse with oneself, that is, to be engaged with that silent dialogue between me and myself' (p. 45), and this was founded upon the sure knowledge that 'whatever else happens, as long as we live we shall have to live together with ourselves' (p. 45).

By drawing out the plurality of the self—contained in the founding theological conceptualisation of the individual, in Mensch's writing, and capable of being read into Arendt's talk of having dialogue with, and living explicitly together with, ourselves—ethics is understood as manifested in the negotiated encounter I have with the presence of others that are empathically part of me. Such an understanding of ethics shares several aspects with Levinas' work. However, it may also help us to avoid those aspects that make his formulations an unlikely foundation for wider engagement with the ethical by critical scholars of organisation. Grounding ethics in the plurality of the individual means that others and the self are not envisaged in binary terms: ethics then is not conceptualised as a kind of violence (Levinas' image of the alterity of the Other invading and persecuting the self), nor is ethical subjectivity envisaged as passivity (Levinas' image of the self compelled by the face of the other against its own wishes). Further, the construction of the idea of individual will and conscience—understood as the fulcrum of Critical Theory and identified by Siedentop, Arendt, Agamben and others as the crucial moral break that Christian theology made from the ancient world—retains a crucial role in the inner negotiation that is ethics. However, this conceptualisation of individual will is not one of an atomistic separateness or sovereignty, but rather plurality. Finally, this understanding of ethics offers a closer affinity between conceptualisations of ethics and politics. Attending to the plurality within ourselves (Arendt's 'silent dialogue between me and myself') in determining our ethical actions is how we seek to engage with difference within and thereby live 'together with ourselves' without being besieged by the clamour of bad conscience. Attending to the plurality of an external other's existence is how we may seek to engage with the political differences between us and try to live together with others. Rather than being conceived as radically different processes, reconceptualising the individual as I have argued for here means that ethics 'shares with politics an acknowledgement of the fundamental human condition: that of plurality' (Mensch 2003:172).

# 6 Conclusion

No one knows who will live in this cage in the future, or whether at the end of this tremendous development entirely new prophets will arise, or there will be a great rebirth of old ideas and ideals, or, if neither, mechanized petrification, embellished with a sort of convulsive self-importance.
Max Weber (1930[2001]:124) *The Protestant Ethic and the Spirit of Capitalism* (© Max Weber. Reproduced with permission of the Licensor through PLSclear)

In the introductory chapter I set out three broad aims for this book. These were to show how theologically resonant concepts were being deployed in current managerial, leadership and organisation discourses; to examine the religious and philosophical roots of these concepts; and to demonstrate how such ideas and languages can be brought into the lexicon of critical organisational scholarship. My hope was that by doing the above, organisational scholars—who have proven themselves very well-schooled in secular ideas but perhaps are rather less used to writing on the theological—can better engage with, critique and reframe non-secular legitimations of neoliberalism and its institutions.

In seeking to do the above through the chapters on *Gods, Devils, Soul* and *The Individual*, I have examined a variety of concepts and discourses. These included religiously inflected discourses of leadership (Servant and Spiritual Leadership and the wider Christian leadership literatures); the historical construction of ethical sovereignty and leaders as sovereign; the demonisation of capitalism and capitalists; modern and ancient understandings of evil and their application to corporate practices in the present; the applicability of the concepts of soul, subjecthood, citizenship and personhood to organisations; the idea of an imperialist corporate soul and the possibility of disciplining it; the category of the individual, its centrality to (neo)liberalism and (in a different form) to criticality; and the individual's religious roots, theological history and philosophical present. In the course of the above, I have engaged with a variety of texts—theological, philosophical, sociological, historical—with some of the key works being those by Arendt, Aristotle, Augustine, Butler, Eagleton, Foucault, Hayek, Kant, Levinas, Liebniz, Locke, Mandeville, Marcuse, Marx, Mensch, Milton, Nietzsche, the New and Old Testaments, Paul, Plato, Siedentop, Smith, Victorian novelists, Voltaire and Weber; as well as business texts, business practices and academic writings on organisation. In the *Introduction*, I wrote that it was my hope that this eclectic assortment of texts and ideas would make an interesting and engaging read and I reiterate that hope here again.

Throughout this book, I have interwoven too an engagement with the question of the nature of our ethical subjectivity—spurred on by my own abiding interest in ethics and an awareness that, for two millennia, the Christian religion has been intimately tied to constructions of who, and what, 'we' as Western subjects are. And so I have used this book to consider whether formative historico-religious foundations might help us to reconceptualise the nature of the ethical subject and its relationship to others. To this end, I examined the idea of 'sovereignty' and 'sovereign individuality', highlighting these as a problematic core in the discourse of leadership; I have shown how the quest for sovereignty has long been understood as a manifestation of evil—even as the *original* evil—and have explored contemporary corporate practices in these terms; I have examined the category of 'the subject', showing how this category contests the idea of ethical sovereignty, but arguing that it does so at the risk of reproducing ethics as wholly *subject to* politics and power; and I have drawn upon founding theological conceptualisations, and recent philosophical writings, to propose that we reconceptualise ethical subjectivity neither as sovereign nor wholly subject to, but rather as a form of *plural individuality* in which the other is always, already, part of the self.

Taken together, the above paragraphs summarise the main concepts, texts and contributions of this work as I see them. And so perhaps the book could end there. That being said, however, I imagine that readers may expect some more thoughts on what I consider the wider implications of this work to be: indeed one of the reviewers of the initial book proposal to Routledge asked for as much. So, I'd like to finish by tracing, tentatively, some possible further implications of what I have examined. I do this by reflecting upon Hugh Willmott's (2013) powerful critique, touched upon in the *Introduction* to this book, of one of the previous 'spirit texts'—namely Boltanski and Chiapello's (2005) *The New Spirit of Capitalism*—as well as by returning one last time to Weber's (1930) *The Protestant Ethic and the Spirit of Capitalism*.

Willmott's central conceptual critique of Boltanski and Chiapello's work, as I see it, is his argument that no new spirit is needed to explain capitalism's ability to endure. Willmott quite rightly says that capitalism for Weber is not a naked system with 'an endemic normative deficit' (p. 120) waiting to be cloaked by successive moral legitimations, legitimations that Boltanski and Chiapello claim to have identified. Rather it is a system already, from the outset, infused with a particular spirit or ethics, 'in the sense of a definite standard of life claiming ethical sanction' (Weber 1930[2001]:23). Willmott defines this ethical sanction as the 'calling to make money' which Weber, as a result of his historico-religious investigations, ascribed a 'quasi-religious meaning and significance' (Willmott 2013:107). 'Developing and safeguarding ways of realizing this calling', rather than inventing a new spirit to remedy a supposed normative deficit, is 'key to capitalism's legitimacy, and thus to its reinvention and reproduction' (ibid). It is, 'this materialist "calling", rather than any other ideological support or justification of this pursuit, that primarily accounts for capitalism's institutionalization and continuation' (p. 105). In Willmott's reading of Weber, this central, dominant, 'calling to make money' is *the* spirit of capitalism, and it is the spirit that drives both capital and labour, owner and employee. So, for Willmott 'the meaningfulness of making money (as income or capital) soon came to displace the meaning of work as a virtue or as a sign of salvation' (p. 104) and

> (s)o long as the means are available to pursue this calling—for example, by creating opportunities for employment, investment, and speculation . . . then critiques of capitalism are absorbed or disarmed before they escalate into widespread, popular demands for radical reform or revolutionary change.
>
> (p. 107)

Through identifying this 'calling to make money' Willmott understands Boltanski and Chiapello to be seeking a solution to the puzzle of capitalism's legitimacy in the lives of its subjects that Weber has already solved. Having taken apart the rationale for Boltanski and Chiapello's entire thesis then, Willmott nevertheless does accept that 'varieties of capitalism are embedded in normative frameworks which enable and constrain their specific form of articulation' (p. 120) and 'that "spirits" and associated ideologies are important in rendering participation in capitalist relations meaningful' (p. 107): just so long as we remember that Weber was 'right to identify and prioritize "the calling of making money"' (p. 107).

So what does Willmott's critique imply for my study? I think, thankfully, that much of these criticisms of Boltanski and Chiapello's 'new spirit' wouldn't linger on how I have been considering religious spirits in the neoliberal present. My work, for example, hasn't sought to make claims about *the* spirit of capitalism, about what these religiously inflected concepts and ideas ultimately mean for capitalism *in toto*. The main contribution of this work, as I see it, has been the detail rather than the destination. I have sought to show some of the religiosity which is again (if it ever really stopped) swirling through and around capitalism and its institutions of work; to still some of these wisps and waifs long enough so that we can better examine and engage with them; and to do this without seeking to distil religious spirits into some grand thesis to be nailed, Martin Luther-like, to the door of the academy. If my work might be regarded as identifying and examining some of the, let's call them *supplementary*, '"spirits" and associated ideologies' that are 'important in rendering participation in capitalist relations meaningful', then I would be very happy with that. This would allow me still to claim that the religious concepts and ideas that I have examined may be both interesting (to me, and I hope to others) and significant. Significant, particularly, when we remember the context of America's dominant Christian faith (estimated by Pew 2015 at 71% of the population, around 230 million people); the sizeable number of evangelical Christians amongst that population (estimated at 25% of the population, around 82 million people); the research identifying this denominational group as providing specific support for neoliberal policies and practices; and the ways that organisational discourses generated in the American context are disseminated, through putatively secular management theory and practice, to other audiences where religiously inflected assumptions and references may be missed. As I say then, I would be very happy with having my study read as contributing to examining supplementary 'spirits and associated ideologies', while having it all still contained within Willmott's admonishment to prioritise Weber's 'calling of making money' as the dominant, underlying spirit.

However, at the risk of reopening a can of worms that has just been neatly shut, it does seem to me that there is a mistake here in the reading of Weber's spirit, a mistake that might have further implications for my text. For it is *not* the case that Weber argues that both capitalists *and* employees are driven by the calling to make money. While some grand declarative passages at the start of the book might seem to suggest this (for instance, 'Man is dominated by the making of money, by acquisition as the ultimate purpose in life' 1930[2001]:18), throughout the text Weber argues that the spirit of capitalism is different for the capitalist as compared to the employee. For those that Weber calls the 'bourgeois businessman' (p. 120), or elsewhere the 'bourgeois-capitalist entrepreneurs' (p. 88), it is indeed a calling to make money which can be understood to define the spirit of capitalism. However, this is not the same spirit which capitalism encapsulates for labour. We can see an example of this in Weber's discussion of piece rates early in his text. The 'modern employer', seeking greater output from employees, may introduce piece rates, 'thereby giving them [the employee] an opportunity to earn what is for them a very high wage' (p. 23). However, rather than raising output in these circumstances, employees frequently reduce it, as 'the opportunity for earning more was less attractive than that of working less' (ibid). Weber cites this as an example of pre-capitalist traditionalism lingering in the consciousness of the workmen. The solution engendered through capitalism to this conundrum is not, however, to bring about in the workman a calling to make money—an overriding imperative to acquisition—such that they would then seek to maximise their piece-rate revenue. Rather, the employee must be 'freed from continual calculations' about the return for their work, and '(l)abour must, on the contrary, be performed as if it were an absolute end in itself, a calling' (p. 24).

This attitude to *labour as a calling* is, as with the bourgeois business-man's calling to make money, traced by Weber back to religious foun-dations. However, where the businessman's spirit had a particularly Calvinist heritage, the worker's was traced back to Protestant Pietism and religious asceticism. For example, Weber writes that, '(t)he power of religious asceticism' provided the businessman 'with sober, conscientious, and unusually industrious workmen, who clung to their work as to a life purpose willed by God' (p. 120). And further,

> we may say that the virtues favoured by Pietism were more those on the one hand of the faithful official, clerk, labourer, or domestic worker. . . . Calvinism, in comparison, appears to be more closely related to the hard legalism and the active enterprise of bourgeois-capitalist entrepreneurs.

Later in the text he writes that 'seen from the side of the workers, the Zinzendorf branch of Pietism, for instance, glorified the loyal worker who did not seek acquisition, but lived according to the apostolic model' (p. 121). He goes on:

> Now naturally the whole ascetic literature of almost all denomina-tions is saturated with the idea that faithful labour, even at low wages, on the part of those whom life offers no other opportunities, is highly pleasing to God. In this respect Protestant Asceticism added in itself nothing new. But it not only deepened this idea most powerfully, it also created the force which was alone decisive for its effectiveness: the psychological sanction of it though the conception of this labour as a calling, as the best, often in the last analysis the only means of attaining certainty of grace.
>
> (ibid)

And, if we are in any doubt of the different callings that the spirit of capitalism made on the businessman and the employee, Weber writes '(t)he treatment of labour as a calling became as characteristic of the modern worker as the corresponding attitude toward acquisition of the business man'. Nowhere does Weber suggest that the employee's calling to labour as an end in itself is transformed into the businessman's calling to continual and ceaseless acquisition—these two ethics are quite distinct aspects of the spirit of capitalism, which provide two different ethical sanctions for these two different classes of subjects. This is not to suggest that the employee's calling to labour as an end in itself remains in some unchangeable state to the present day. Weber argued that the importance of the calling to labour as the mobilising basis for employee participation in capitalism had come to be largely subsumed within the 'technical and economic conditions of machine production which to-day determine the lives of all the individuals who are born into this mechanism' (p. 123). And, as we saw in Chapter 5 *The Individual*, this theme of employees being subordinated to the dictates of a machine rationality continues beyond Weber into a range of works throughout the twentieth century, including Marcuse's (1941) *Some Social Implications of Modern Technology*, C. W. Mills' (1951) *White Collar*, Whyte's (1956) *Organization Man*, Braverman's (1974) *Labour and Monopoly Capital*, and Bauman's (1989) *Modernity and The Holocaust*.

So, where does all this get us and what bearing does this have on my examination of religiosity and neoliberalism? Well, when we remember that the spirit of capitalism that mobilised employees, this calling to labour as an end in itself, was understood to have been subsumed within the 'technical and economic conditions of machine production', we might need to reconsider what happens to the 'spirit' when the discipline and schedule of machine production no longer dominates economic life. What happens when, for example, there is widespread outsourcing of industrial and manufacturing jobs to 'developing' economies, reducing the experience for many Americans of being daily subjected to machine rationality and the discipline of mechanised production; when there is the rise of financialisation and financialised capitalism, characterised by intangible, invisible, unknowable and seemingly capricious entities determining our lives; when large-scale casualisation and precarity bring great levels of ambiguity into working lives, reducing the sustained disciplinary effects of a career in either factory or office; when the dominance of service-based work requires a manufactured-authentic love of one's neighbour and a turning of the other cheek when continual cost-cutting produces an ever-frustrated customer base; when the reality of irrepressible climate change heralds the threat of apocalyptic floods, fires, exodus or plagues? And what happens when on top of all of this, rather than the mechanical materiality of Fordism, the circuitry of the computer and the immateriality of the internet or 'cloud' dominate: an intangible, floating, web that is everywhere and nowhere; that is constantly watching us in minute detail; that is always with us in the p(s)alm-sized phones we show such deep devotion to; that is governed by impossibly distant leaders of unimaginably vast institutions, beings who are already being represented in ways suggestive of deification?

The sorts of changes listed above do seem to me to be dismantling sites of industrialised machine production, and carriers of mechanistic rationalities, for much of the US and wider Western working populations. I have highlighted Weber's argument that it was in such mechanised sites and rationalities where the employees' spirit of capitalism—labour as a calling—had been subsumed. And I have suggested that the neoliberal present, with its precarious employment, financialisation, inequalities, climate change and cloud-based modalities, ushers in an experience of invisible distant powers, of profound uncertainty, ambiguity and intangibility, even of apocalyptic threat, for the working population. What spirits, ideas, or institutions will people turn to try and make sense of the above? There are, of course, a variety of possibilities. To my mind, however, these are the sort of conditions that may well generate further propensity for a dominantly Christian population to turn towards religiosity as a means of understanding and accommodating themselves to the neoliberal capitalist present—to turn towards institutions and discourses with long resonance to an experience of invisible distant powers, intangibility, the ambiguous, even the apocalyptic. I'm not suggesting that this heralds a 'new spirit of capitalism' perhaps. But it does seem to set up prime conditions for further invocation of religious spirits to make sense of and legitimise the organisation of work in the neoliberal present—spirits which critical scholars of organisation will need to engage with, as this book has sought to do, with attentiveness to their theological and philosophical inflections.

# References

Adams, G. and Balfour, D. (1998) *Unmasking Administrative Evil*. London, Sage.

Adams, J. (1992) 'The corporation versus the market' *Journal of Economic Issues* 26(2): 397–405.

Agamben, G. (2011) *The Kingdom and the Glory: For a Theological Genealogy of Economy and Government*. Stanford, Stanford University Press.

Ailon, G. (2013) 'From superstars to devils: The ethical discourse on managerial figures involved in a corporate scandal' *Organization* 22(1): 78–99.

Anderson, D. and Maxwell, J. (2009) *How to Run Your Business by the Book: A Biblical Blueprint to Bless Your Business*. Hoboken, NJ, Wiley.

Antonakis, J., Fenley, M. and Liechti, S. (2012) 'Learning Charisma' *Harvard Business Review* 90(6): 127–130.

Arendt, H. (1951) *The Origins of Totalitarianism*. New York, Schocken Books.

Arendt, H. (1963[2006]) *Eichmann in Jerusalem: A Report on the Banality of Evil*. London, Penguin Books.

Arendt, H. (1964a) '"Eichmann in Jerusalem": An exchange of letters between Gershom Scholem and Hannah Arendt' *Encounter*, January: 51–56.

Arendt, H. (1964b) 'Personal responsibility under a dictatorship.' Available at https://grattoncourses.files.wordpress.com/2017/07/arendt-personal-responsibility-under-a-dictatorship.pdf

Arendt, H. (1971a[2003]) 'Thinking and moral considerations' in J. Kohn (Ed.) *Responsibility and Judgement*. New York, Schocken Books, pp. 159–189.

Arendt, H. (1971b) *The Life of the Mind*. San Diego, Harcourt Brace Jovanovich.

Arnold, D. (2006) 'Corporate moral agency' *Midwest Studies in Philosophy* 30: 279–291.

Ashley, D. and Sandefer, R. (2013) 'Neoliberalism and the privatization of welfare and religious organizations in the United States of America' in T. Martikainen and F. Gauthier (Eds.) *Religion in the Neoliberal Age: Politics, Economy and Modes of Governance*. London, Routledge, pp. 109–128.

Ashmos, D. and Duchon, D. (2000) 'Spirituality at work: A conceptualization and measure' *Journal of Management Inquiry* 9(2): 134–145.

Augustine. (400[1961]) *Confessions*, trns. F. J. Sheed, Andrews and McMeel.

Augustine. (427[1972]) *City of God*, trns. H. Bettenson. Harmodsworth, Penguin.

Avolio, B. and Gardner, W. (2005) 'Authentic leadership development' *Leadership Quarterly* 16: 315–338.

Avolio, B., Gardner, W., Walumba, F., Luthans, F. and May, D. (2004) 'Unlocking the mask: A look at the process by which authentic leaders impact follower attitudes and behaviours' *Leadership Quarterly* 15: 801–823.

Bakan, J. (2004) *The Corporation*. London, Constable.

Banerjee, S. B. (2007) *Corporate Social Responsibility*. Cheltenham, Edward Elgar.

Baratz, M. (1970) *The American Business System in Transition*. New York, Cromwell.

Bardon, T. and Josserand, E. (2011) 'A Nietzschean reading of Foucauldian thinking: Constructing a project of the self within an ontology of becoming' *Organization* 18(4): 497–515.

Bass, B. (1985) *Leadership and Performance beyond Expectations*. New York, Free Press.

Bass, B. and Avolio, B. (1993) 'Transformational leadership: A response to critiques' in M. Chemers and R. Ayman (Eds.) *Leadership Theory and Research*. New York, Academic Press.

Bass, B. and Steidlmeier, P. (1999) 'Ethics, character and authentic transformational leadership behaviour' *Leadership Quarterly* 10(2): 181–217.

Batstone, D. (2003) *Saving the Corporate Soul & (Who Knows?) Maybe Your Own: Eight Principles for Creating and Preserving Integrity and Profitability without Selling Out*. San Francisco, Jossey-Bass.

Bauman, Z. (1989[1991]) *Modernity and the Holocaust*. Cambridge, Polity Press.

Bauman, Z. (2001) *Community*. Cambridge, Polity Press.

Beal, T. (2002) *Religion and Its Monsters*. London, Routledge.

Beausay, W. (2009) *The Leadership Genius of Jesus: Ancient Wisdom for Modern Business*. Nashville, TN, Thomas Nelson.

Bell, E. and Taylor, S. (2003) 'The elevation of work: Pastoral power and the new age work ethic' *Organization* 10(2): 329–349.

Bell, E. and Taylor, S. (2004) 'From outward bound to inward bound: The prophetic voices and discursive practices of spiritual management development' *Human Relations* 57(4): 439–466.

Bell, E. and Taylor, S. (2016) 'Spirituality, religion and organization' in R. Mir, H. Willmott and M. Greenwood (Eds.) *The Routledge Companion to Philosophy in Organization Studies*. Oxon, Routledge, pp. 550–558.

Bell, E., Taylor, S. and Driscoll, C. (2012) 'Varieties of organizational soul: The ethics of belief in organizations' *Organization* 19(4): 425–439.

Bellingham, R. (2009) *Creating Organizational Soul: The Source of Positive Change and Transformation*. Amherst, MA, HRD Press.

Benefiel, M. (2008) *The Soul of a Leader: Finding Your Path to Fulfilment and Success*. New York, Crossroad Publishing.

Benhabib, S. (1992) 'The generalised and the concrete other' in E. Frazer, J. Hornsby and S. Lovibond (Eds.) *Ethics: A Feminist Reader*. Oxford, Blackwell, pp. 267–300.

Berger, P. (1999) 'The desecularization of the world: A global overview' in P. Berger (Ed.) *The Desecularization of the World: Resurgent Religion and World Politics*. Washington, DC, Ethics and Public Policy Center, and Grand Rapids, Mich., W. B. Eerdmans Publishing Co., pp. 1–18.

Berlin, I. (1990) *The Crooked Timber of Humanity: Chapters in the History of Ideas*, ed. H. Hardy. London, John Murray.

Bevan, E. and Corvellec, H. (2007) 'The impossibility of corporate ethics: For a Levinasian approach to managerial ethics' *Business Ethics: A European Review* 16(3): 208–219.

Blanchard, K. (2010) *The Protestant Ethic or the Spirit of Capitalism*. Eugene, Oregon, Cascade Books.

Blanchard, K. and Hodges, P. (2003) *Servant Leader: Transforming Your Heart, Heads, Hands and Habits*. Nashville, TN, Thomas Nelson.

Blanchard, K. and Hodges, P. (2008) *Lead Like Jesus: Lessons from the Greatest Leadership Role Model of All Time*. Nashville, TN, Thomas Nelson.

Blanchard, K., Hodges, P. and Hendry, P. (2016) *Lead Like Jesus Revisited: Lessons from the Greatest Leadership Role Model of All Time*. Nashville, TN, Thomas Nelson.

Blanchard, K. and Johnson, S. (1982) *The One Minute Manager*. New York, William Morrow and Company.

Bolman, L. G. and Deal, T. E. (1995) *Leading with Soul: An Uncommon Journey of Spirit*. San Francisco, CA, Jossey Bass.

Boltanski, L. and Chiapello, E. (1999[2005]) *The New Spirit of Capitalism*. London, Verso.

Bookstaber, R. (2007) *A Demon of Our Own Design: Markets, Hedge Funds, and the Perils of Financial Innovation*. Hoboken, NJ, Wiley.

Bowler, K. (2015) 'The daily grind: The spiritual workday of the American Prosperity Gospel' *Journal of Cultural Economy* 8(5): 630–636.

Braverman, H. (1974) *Labour and Monopoly Capital*. London, Monthly Review Press.

Brilliant, R. (1991) *Portraiture*. London, Reaktion Books.

Briner, B. (2005) *The Management Methods of Jesus*. Nashville, TN, Thomas Nelson.

Briner, B. and Pritchard, R. (2008) *Leadership Lessons of Jesus*. Nashville, TN, B & H Publishing.

Brown, T. (1995) 'On the Edge: Jesus CEO?' *Industry Week* March 6: 14–20.

Butler, J. (1997) *The Psychic Life of Power*. Stanford, Stanford University Press.

Butler, J. (2005) *Giving an Account of Oneself*. New York, Fordham University Press.

Byers, D. and Rhodes, C. (2007) 'Ethics, alterity, and organizational justice' *Business Ethics: A European Review* 16(3): 239–250.

Cadava, E., Connor, P. and Nancy, J. (Eds.) (1991) *Who Comes after the Subject?* London, Routledge.

Calàs, M. and Smircich, L. (1991) 'Voicing seduction to silence leadership' *Organization Studies* 12(4): 567–602.

Campbell, C. (2005) *The Romantic Ethic and the Spirit of Modern Consumerism*, Third Edition. York, Alcuin Academics.

Card, C. (2002) *The Atrocity Paradigm: A Theory of Evil*. Oxford, Oxford University Press.

Cardone, M. (2009) *Business with Soul: Creating a Workplace Rich in Faith and Values*. Nashville, Thomas Nelson.

Carlyle, T. (1841) *On Heroes, Hero-Worship and the Heroic in History*. London, James Fraser.

Chappell, T. (1996) *The Soul of a Business*. New York, NY, Bantam.

Chodorow, N. (1986) 'Towards a relational individualism: The mediation of self through psychoanalysis' in T. Heller, M. Sosna and D. Wellbery (Eds.)

*Reconstructing Individualism: Autonomy, Individuality, and the Self in Western Thought*. Stanford, Stanford University Press, pp. 197–207.

Cole, P. (2006) *The Myth of Evil: Demonizing the Enemy*. London, Praeger.

Coles, R. (1992) *Self/Power/Other*. London, Cornell University Press.

Collins, H. and Wray-Bliss, E. (2005) 'Discriminating ethics' *Human Relations* 58(6): 799–824.

Collinson, D. (1994) 'Strategies of resistance: Power, knowledge and subjectivity in the workplace' in J. Jermier, D. Knights and W. Nord (Eds.) *Resistance and Power in Organizations: Agency, Subjectivity and the Labour Process*. London, Routledge, pp. 25–68.

Conger, J. (2011) 'Charismatic leadership' in A. Bryman, et al. (Eds.) *The Sage Handbook of Leadership*. London, Sage, pp. 86–102.

Conlin, M. (1999) 'Religion in the workplace: The growing presence of spirituality in corporate America' *Business Week*, November, 3653: 150.

Cooke, B. (2003) 'The denial of slavery in management studies' *Journal of Management Studies* 40(8): 1895–1918.

Coser, L. (1974) *Greedy Institutions: Patterns of Undivided Commitment*. New York, Free Press.

Cox, A. and Liesse, J. (1996) *Redefining Corporate Soul: Linking Purpose and People*. Chicago, IL, Irwin Professional Publishing.

Critchley, S. (2007) *Infinitely Demanding: Ethics of Commitment, Politics of Resistance*. London, Verso.

Davis, M. (2011) *The Soul of the Greeks*. Chicago, University of Chicago Press.

De Georges, O. (1791) *Declaration of the Rights of Woman and Citizen*. Available at www.fmyv.es/ci/in/women/3.pdf

Derrida, J. (1991) '"Eating well," on the calculation of the subject: An interview with Jacques Derrida' in E. Cadava, P. Connor and J. Nancy (Eds.) *Who Comes after the Subject?* New York and London, Routledge, pp. 96–119.

Du Gay, P. and Morgan, G. (Eds.) (2013) *New Spirits of Capitalism? Crises, Justifications, and Dynamics*. Oxford, Oxford University Press.

Du Gay, P. and Salaman, G. (1992) 'The cult(ure) of the customer' *Journal of Management Studies* 29(5): 615–633.

Eagleton, T. (2005) *The English Novel*. Oxford, Blackwell Publishing.

Eagleton, T. (2010) *On Evil*. New Haven, Yale University Press.

Fairholm, G. (1996) 'Spiritual leadership: Fulfilling whole-self needs at work' *Leadership & Organization Development Journal* 17(5): 11–17.

Fairhurst, G. and Grant, D. (2010) 'The social construction of leadership: A sailing guide' *Management Communication Quarterly* 24(2): 171–210.

Fernando, M. (2011) 'Spirituality and leadership' in A. Bryman, D. Collinson, K. Grint, B. Jackson and M. Ulh-Bien (Eds.) *The Sage Handbook of Leadership*. London, Sage, pp. 483–494.

Feuerbach, L. (1890) *The Essence of Christianity*, trns. M. Evans, Second Edition. London, Kegan Paul, Trench, Trubner, and Co, Ltd. Available at www.gutenberg.org/files/47025/47025-h/47025-h.htm#s1.2

Flanagan, W. (2003) *Dirty Rotten CEOs*. Rowville, Australia, The Five Mile Press.

Flowers, K. (2014) *The Soul of Business: How to Create and Sustain the Right Culture in Your Company*. Denver, CO, Outskirts Press Inc.

Ford, J. and Harding, N. (2003) 'Invoking Satan or the ethics of the employment contract' *Journal of Management Studies* 40(5): 1131–1150.

Ford, J. and Harding, N. (2011) 'The impossibility of the "true self" of authentic leadership' *Leadership* 7(4): 463–479.

Forsythe, N. (1987) *The Old Enemy: Satan and the Combat Myth*. Princeton, NJ, Princeton University Press.

Foucault, M. (1965[1988]) *Madness and Civilisation*. New York, Vintage Books and Random House.

Foucault, M. (1975[1995]) *Discipline and Punish: The Birth of the Prison*, trns. A. Sheridan. New York, Random House.

Foucault, M. (1978) *The History of Sexuality*, trns. R. Hurley, Volume 1. New York, Pantheon.

Foucault, M. (1984) *The Foucault Reader*, ed. P. Rabinow. New York, Random House.

Foucault, M. (1993) 'About the beginning of the hermeneutics of the self' *Political Theory* 21(2): 198–227.

Foucault, M. (2001) *Fearless Speech*. Los Angeles, Semiotext(e).

Foucault, M. (2005) *The Hermeneutics of the Subject*. New York, Picador.

Foucault, N. (1963[1994]) *The Birth of the Clinic*. New York, Vintage Books and Random House.

French, P. (1979) 'The corporation as moral person' *American Philosophical Quarterly* 16(3): 207–215.

French, P. (2014) 'Corporate moral agency' *Wiley Encyclopaedia of Management*. Available at https://onlinelibrary.wiley.com/doi/abs/10.1002/9781118785317.weom020062

Friedman, M. (1962) *Capitalism and Freedom*. Chicago, IL, University of Chicago Press.

Friend, T. (2017) 'The god pill' *The New Yorker*, April 3: 54.

Fry, L. (2003) 'Toward a theory of spiritual leadership' *The Leadership Quarterly* 14: 693–727.

Fry, L., Vitucci, S. and Cedillo, M. (2005) 'Spiritual leadership and army transformation: Theory, measurement, and establishing a baseline' *The Leadership Quarterly* 16: 835–862.

Gabriel, Y. (1997) 'Meeting God: When organizational members come face to face with the supreme leader' *Human Relations* 50(4): 315–342.

Gallagher, R. S. (2002) *The Soul of an Organization: Understanding the Values That Drive Successful Corporate Cultures*. Chicago, IL, Dearborn Trade Publishing.

Garber, M., Hanssen, B. and Walkowitz, R. (Eds.) (2000) *The Turn to Ethics*. London, Routledge.

Gardner, W., Avolio, B. and Luthans, F. (2005) 'Can you see the real me? A self based model of authentic leader and follower development' *Leadership Quarterly* 16: 343–372.

Gaulthier, F., Martikainen, T. and Woodhead, L. (2013) 'Introduction: Religion in market society' in T. Martikainen and F. Gauthier (Eds.) *Religion in the Neoliberal Age: Politics, Economy and Modes of Governance*. London, Routledge, pp. 1–20.

Gemmill, G. and Oakley, J. (1992) 'Leadership: An alienating social myth' *Human Relations* 45(2): 113–129.

Giacalone, R. A. (2010) 'JMSR: Where are we now-where are we going?' *Journal of Management, Spirituality and Religion* 7(1): 3–6.

Giacalone, R. A. and Jurkiewicz, C. L. (Eds.) (2003) *Handbook of Workplace Spirituality and Organizational Performance*. New York, NY, M.E. Sharpe.

Glover, J. (1999) *Humanity: A Moral History of the Twentieth Century*. London, Jonathan Cape.

Goodpaster, K. and Matthews, J. (1982) 'Can a corporation have a conscience?' *Harvard Business Review*, January Issue.

Gordon, R. (2010) 'Dispersed leadership: Exploring the impact of antecedent forms of power using a communicative framework' *Management Communication Quarterly* 24(2): 260–287.

Gorski, P., Kyuman Kim, D., Torpey, J. and VanAntwerpen, J. (2012) 'Introduction: The post secular in question' in P. Gorski, D. Kyuman Kim, J. Torpey and J. VanAntwerpen (Eds.) *The Post Secular in Question: Religion in Contemporary Society*. New York, NY, New York University Press, pp. 1–22.

Gramm, W. (1989) 'Oligarchic capitalism' in M. Tool and W. Samuels (Eds.) *State, Society and Corporate Power*. Oxford, Transaction Publishers, pp. 353–374.

Greenblatt, S. (1986) 'Fiction and friction' in T. Heller, M. Sosna and D. Wellbery (Eds.) *Reconstructing Individualism: Autonomy, Individuality, and the Self in Western Thought*. Stanford, Stanford University Press, pp. 30–52.

Greenfeld, L. (2001) *The Spirit of Capitalism: Nationalism and Economic Growth*. Cambridge, MA, Harvard University Press.

Greenleaf, R. (1970) *The Servant as Leader*. Available at www.greenleaf.org

Greenpeace (n.d.) 'Exxon's climate Denial history: A timeline.' Available at www. greenpeace.org/usa/global-warming/exxon-and-the-oil-industry-knew-about-climate-change/exxons-climate-denial-history-a-timeline/

Grey, C. (1994) 'Career as a project of the self and labour process discipline' *Sociology* 28: 479–497.

Griffith, V. (1997) 'The business angels: Executives-particularly in the US-are bringing religion to work' *Financial Times*, January 18: 9.

Grint, K. (1995) *Management: A Sociological Introduction*. Cambridge, Polity.

Grint, K. (2010) 'The sacred in leadership' *Organization Studies* 31(1): 89–107.

Grint, K. (2011) 'The history of leadership' in A. Bryman, et al. (Eds.) *The Sage Handbook of Leadership*. London, Sage, pp. 3–14.

The Guardian (2018) 'ACTU report shows half Australian workers will soon be casual' *The Guardian*, May 21. Available at www.theguardian.com

Gunther, M. (2001) 'God and business' *Fortune* 144(1): 58.

Hackworth, J. (2013) 'Faith, welfare and the formation of the modern American right' in T. Martikainen and F. Gauthier (Eds.) *Religion in the Neoliberal Age: Politics, Economy and Modes of Governance*. London, Routledge, pp. 91–108.

Hall, S. (2015) 'Exxon knew about climate change almost 40 years ago' *Scientific American*, October 26.

Harari, Y. (2016) *Homo Deus: A Brief History of Tomorrow*. London, Harvill Secker.

Harvey, D. (2005) *A Brief History of Neoliberalism*. Oxford, Oxford University Press.

Hayek, F. A. (1967) 'Dr. Bernard Mandeville: Lecture on a Master Mind' *Proceedings of the British Academy*. London.

Hayek, L. (1960[2006]) *The Constitution of Liberty*. London and New York, Routledge Classics.

Hedges, C. (2006) *American Fascists: The Christian Right and the War on America*. New York, Free Press.

Hegel, G. W. F. (1806) *Philosophie des Geistes* (Philosophy of spirit), trns. in Leo Rauch (1983) *Hegel and the Human Spirit*. Detroit, Wayne State University Press.

Hegel, G. W. F. (1807[1977]) *Phänomenologie des Geistes* (Phenomenology of spirit). Oxford, Oxford University Press.

Heller, T. and Wellbery, D. (1986) 'Introduction' in T. Heller, M. Sosna and D. Wellbery (Eds.) *Reconstructing Individualism: Autonomy, Individuality, and the Self in Western Thought*. Stanford, Stanford University Press, pp. 1–15.

Herod, A. and Lambert, R. (2016) 'Neoliberalism, precarious work and remarking the geography of global capitalism' in R. Lambert and A. Herod (Eds.) *Neoliberal Capitalism and Precarious Work: Ethnographies of Accommodation and Resistance*. Cheltenham, Edward Elgar, pp. 1–41.

Hill, L. (2001) 'The hidden theology of Adam Smith' *European Journal of the History of Economic Thought* 8(1): 1–29 in P. Oslington (Ed.) *The International Library of Critical Writings in Economics 167: Economics and Religion*, Volume 1. Cheltenham, Edward Elgar, pp. 292–320.

Hochschild, A. (1983) *The Managed Heart*. Berkeley, University of California Press.

Horkheimer, M. (1941[2005]) 'The end of reason' in A. Arato and E. Gebhardt (Eds.) *The Essential Frankfurt School Reader*. London, Continuum, pp. 26–48.

Jackall, R. (1988) *Moral Mazes: The World of Corporate Managers*. Oxford, Oxford University Press.

Jackson, B. and Parry, K. (2011) *A Very Short, Fairly Interesting and Reasonably Cheap Book about Studying Leadership*. London, Sage.

Jacques. P., Dunlap, R. and Freeman, M. (2008) 'The organisation of denial: Conservative think tanks and environmental scepticism' *Environmental Politics* 17(3): 349–385.

Jaffee, D. (2001) *Organization Theory: Tension and Change*. Boston, MA, McGraw Hill.

John Paul II (1998) 'The holy spirit: Soul of the church' *General Audience*. Available at www.piercedhearts.org/jpii/general_audiences/gen_aud_1998/july_08_98.htm

Johnson, M. (2006) *CEO for God, Family and Country*. Lincoln, NB, iUniverse.

Jones, C. (2003) 'As if business ethics were possible, "within such limits"' *Organization* 10: 223–248.

Jones, C. (2007) 'Editorial introduction' *Business Ethics: A European Review* 16(3): 196–202.

Jones, C., Parker, M. and ten Bos, R. (2005) *For Business Ethics: A Critical Approach*. Abingdon, Routledge.

Jones, L. (1996) *Jesus CEO: Using Ancient Wisdom for Visionary Leadership*. New York, Hyperion.

Julian, L. (2002) *God Is My CEO: Following God's Principles in a Bottom Line World*. Avon, MA, Adams Media.

Kaplan, E. (2004) *With God on Their Side: George W Bush and the Christian Right*. New York, The New Press.

Kaulingfreks, R. and ten Bos, R. (2001) 'Learning to fly: Inspiration and togetherness' *Electronic Journal of Radical Organisation Theory* 7(2): 1–16.

Kaulingfreks, R. and ten Bos, R. (2007) 'On faces and defacement: The case of Kate Moss' *Business Ethics: A European Review* 16(3): 302–312.

Kelly, P., Allender, S. and Colquhoun, D. (2007) 'New work ethics? The corporate athlete's back end index and organizational performance' *Organization* 14(2): 267–285.

Kets de Vries, M. F. (1991) *Organizations on the Couch: Clinical Perspectives on Organizational Behavior and Change*. New York, Jossey-Bass.

Kets de Vries, M. F. and Balazs, K. (2011) 'The Shadow side of leadership' in A. Bryman, et al. (Eds.) *The Sage Handbook of Leadership*. London, Sage, pp. 380–392.

Klein, N. (2000) *No Logo*. London, Flamingo.

Knights, D. (1990) 'Subjectivity, power and the labour process' in D. Knights and H. Willmott (Eds.) *Labour Process Theory*. London, Macmillan.

Knights, D. (1997) 'Organization theory in the age of deconstruction: Dualism, gender and postmodernism revisited' *Organization Studies* 18(1): 1–19.

Knights, D. and Vurdubakis, T. (1994) 'Foucault, power, resistance and all that' in J. Jermier, D. Knights and W. Nord (Eds.) *Resistance and Power in Organizations: Agency, Subjectivity and the Labour Process*. London, Routledge, pp. 167–198.

Knights, D. and Willmott, H. (1989) 'Power and subjectivity at work: From degradation to subjugation in social relations' *Sociology* 23(4): 535–558.

Koehn, D. (2000) 'Traversing the *Inferno*: A new direction for business ethics' *Business Ethics Quarterly* 10(1): 255–268.

Koehn, D. (2007) 'Facing the phenomenon of evil' *International Management Review* 3(1): 38–49.

Kosmin, B. and Keysar, A. (2009) *American Religious Identification Survey (ARIS): Summary Report*. Available at www.americanreligionsurvey-aris.org

Kottasova, I. (2016) 'How Apple paid just 0.005% tax on its global profits' *CNN Money, London*. Available at www.money.cnn.com

Kristeva, J. (2001) *Hannah Arendt*, trns. R. Güberman. New York, Columbia University Press.

Kunda, G. (2006) *Engineering Culture*. Philadelphia, Temple University Press.

Lampert, M. (2016) 'Corporate social responsibility and the supposed moral agency of corporations' *Ephemera* 16(1): 79–105.

Laski, H. (1936) *The Rise of European Liberalism*. London, Routledge.

Lehman, C. (2016) 'How the prosperity gospel explains Donald Trump's popularity with Christian voters' *The Washington Post*, July 15.

Levinas, E. (1969) *Totality and Infinity*. Pittsburgh, Duquesne University Press.

Levinas, E. (1974[1998]) *Otherwise Than Being: Or beyond Essence*. Pittsburgh, Duquesne University Press.

Lizardo, O. (2009) 'The Devil as cognitive mapping' *Rethinking Marxism* 21(4): 605–618.

Locke, J. (1690[1980]) *Second Treatise on Government*, ed. C. B. McPherson. Cambridge, Hackett. Available at www.gutenberg.org/files/7370/7370-h/7370-h.htm

Lodge, D. (1966) *Language of Fiction: Essays in Criticism and Verbal Analysis of the English Novel*. London, Routledge and Kegan Paul.

Loewenstein, D. (2004) *Milton: Paradise Lost*. Cambridge, Cambridge University Press.

Lorenz, H. (2009) 'Ancient theories of soul' in E. Zalta (Ed.) *The Stanford Encyclopaedia of Philosophy*. Available at http://plato.stanford.edu/archives/sum2009/entries/ancient-soul/

MacIntyre, A. (1985) *After Virtue*, Second Edition. London, Duckworth.

Mandeville, B. (1723) *The Fable of the Bees: Or Private Vices, Public Benefits*. Loschberg, Germany, Jazzybee-Verlag.

Marchand, R. (1998) *Creating the Corporate Soul*. Berkeley, CA, University of California Press.

Marcuse, H. (1941[2005]) 'Some social implications of modern technology' in A. Arato and E. Gebhardt (Eds.) *The Essential Frankfurt School Reader*. London, Continuum, pp. 138–162.

Marcuse, H. (1964) *One Dimensional Man*. London, Routledge and Kegan Paul.

Martikainen, T. (2013) 'Multilevel and pluricentric network governance of religion' in T. Martikainen and F. Gauthier (Eds.) *Religion in the Neoliberal Age: Politics, Economy and Modes of Governance*. London, Routledge, pp. 129–142.

Marx, K. (1843[2012]) *On the Jewish Question*. Chicago, IL, Aristeus Books.

Marx, K. (1844a[1992]) 'Economic and philosophic manuscripts' in *Karl Marx Early Writings*, trns. R. Livingstone and G. Benton. London, Penguin Books, pp. 279–400.

Marx, K. (1844b[1992]) 'A contribution to the critique of Hegel's philosophy of right' in *Karl Marx Early Writings*, trns. R. Livingstone and G. Benton. London, Penguin Books, pp. 243–258.

Marx, K. (1845) 'Thesis on Feuerbach' in *Karl Marx Early Writings*, trns. R. Livingstone and G. Benton. London, Penguin Books, pp. 421–423.

Marx, K. (1852) *The Eighteenth Brumaire of Louis Bonaparte*. Available at www.marxist.org

Marx, K. (1867[1990]) *Capital: Volume 1*. London, Penguin Books.

Marx, K. and Engels, F. (1845[1932]) *The German Ideology: Introduction to a Critique of Political Economy*. London, Lawrence and Wishart.

Matthews, G. (1992) *Thought's Ego in Augustine and Descartes*. New York, Cornell University Press.

McCabe, D. (2000) 'Factory innovations and management machinations: The productive and repressive relations of power' *Journal of Management Studies* 37(7): 931–953.

McDonald, L. and Robinson, P. (2009) *A Colossal Failure of Common Sense*. London, Ebury Press.

McLean, B. and Elkind, P. (2003) *The Smartest Guys in the Room*. New York, Penguin Books.

McLean, B. and Nocera, J. (2010) *All the Devils Are Here*. New York, Penguin Books.

McLellan, G. (2007) 'Towards a postsecular sociology?' *Sociology* 41(5): 857–870.

McMurray, R., Pullen, A. and Rhodes, C. (2011) 'Ethical subjectivity and politics in organizations: A case of health care tendering' *Organization* 18(4): 541–561.

Meindl, J., Ehrlich, S. and Dukerich, J. (1985) 'The romance of leadership' *Administrative Science Quarterly* 30(1): 78–102.

Mendelson, M. (2012) 'Saint Augustine' in E. Zalta (Ed.) *The Stanford Encyclopaedia of Philosophy*. Available at http://plato.stanford.edu/archives/win2012/entries/augustine/

Mensch, J. (2003) *Ethics and Selfhood: Alterity and the Phenomenology of Obligation*. New York, State University of New York Press.

Messadié, G. (1996) *Historie Générale du Diable*, trns. M. Romano. London, Kodansha International.

Meyer, J. (1986) 'Myths of socialization and of personality' in T. Heller, M. Sosna and D. Wellbery (Eds.) *Reconstructing Individualism: Autonomy, Individuality, and the Self in Western Thought*. Stanford, Stanford University Press, pp. 208–221.

Milbank, J. (1990) 'Political economy as theodicy and agnostics' in *Theology and Social Theory: Beyond Secular Reason*. Oxford, Blackwell Publishing, pp. 27–48 in P. Oslington (Ed.) *The International Library of Critical Writings in Economics 167: Economics and Religion*, Volume 1. Cheltenham, Edward Elgar, pp. 266–287.

Milgram, S. (1974) *Obedience to Authority: An Experimental View*. New Haven, Yale University Press.

Miller, P. and O'Leary, T. (1987) 'Accounting and the construction of the governable person' *Accounting, Organizations and Society* 12(3): 235–265.

Mills, C. W. (1951) *White Collar*. Oxford, Oxford University Press.

Mills, C. W. (1956) *The Power Elite*. New York, Oxford University Press.

Milton, J. (1667[2000]) *Paradise Lost*. London, Penguin Books.

Mitroff, I. I. and Denton, E. A. (1999) *A Spiritual Audit of Corporate America: A Hard Look at Spirituality, Religion and Values in the Workplace*. San Francisco, CA, Jossey-Bass Publishers.

Mont Pelerin Society (1947) 'Statement of aims.' Available at www.montpelerin.org

Moon, J. (1995) 'The firm as citizen?' *Australian Journal of Political Science* 30: 1–17.

Moore, G. (1999) 'Corporate moral agency: Review and implications' *Journal of Business Ethics* 21: 329–343.

Moreton, B. (2010) *To Serve God and Wal-Mart: The Making of Christian Free Enterprise*. Cambridge, MA, Harvard University Press.

Nash, L. (1994) *Believers in Business*. London, Thomas.

Neal, J. and Biberman, J. (2003) 'Introduction: The leading edge in research on spirituality and organizations' *Journal of Organizational Change Management* 16(4): 363–366.

Neiman, S. (1994) *The Unity of Reason: Rereading Kant*. New York and Oxford, Oxford University Press.

Neiman, S. (2002) *Evil in Modern Thought: An Alternative History of Philosophy*. Princeton, Princeton University Press.

Nelson, R. (1993) 'The theological meaning of economics' *Christian Century* 110(23): 777–781 in P. Oslington (Ed.) *The International Library of Critical Writings in Economics 167: Economics and Religion*, Volume 1. Cheltenham, Edward Elgar, pp. 502–506.

Ngai, P. and Huilin, L. (2016) 'Constructing violence and resistance: The political economy of the construction industry and labour subcontracting system in post-socialist China' in R. Lambert and A. Herod (Eds.) *Neoliberal Capitalism and Precarious Work: Ethnographies of Accommodation and Resistance*. Edward Elgar, Cheltenham, pp. 125–147.

Nietzsche, F. (1878[2006]) 'Human all too human' in K. Pearson and D. Large (Eds.) *The Nietzsche Reader*. Oxford, Blackwell, pp. 161–190.

Nietzsche, F. (1886[2006]) 'Beyond good and evil' in K. Pearson and D. Large (Eds.) *The Nietzsche Reader*. Oxford, Blackwell, pp. 311–361.

Nietzsche, F. (1887[1996]) *On the Genealogy of Morals: A Polemic*, trns. D. Smith. Oxford, Oxford University Press.

Nietzsche, F. (1887[2007]) *On the Genealogy of Morality*, trns. C. Diethe. Cambridge, Cambridge University Press.

Norris, P. and Inglehart, R. (2004) *Sacred and Secular: Religion and Politics Worldwide*. New York, Cambridge University Press.

Novak, M. (1993) *The Catholic Ethic and the Spirit of Capitalism*. New York, The Free Press.

Novak, M. (1982) *The Spirit of Democratic Capitalism*. New York, Simon and Schuster.

O'Flynn, M. (2009) *Profitable Ideas: The Ideology of the Individual in Capitalist Development*. Boston, Brill Academic Publishers.

Ogunlaru, R. (2012) *Soul Trader: Putting the Heart Back Into Your Business*. London/ Philadelphia, Kogan Paul Limited.

Olson, L. (2007) 'Religious affiliations, political preferences, and ideological alignments' in J. Beckford and N. Demerath (Eds.) *The Sage Handbook of the Sociology of Religion*. London, Sage, pp. 438–457.

Oxfam (2016) 'The Hidden Billions: How tax havens impact lives at home and abroad' *Oxfam Research Reports*. Available at www.oxfam.org

Oxfam (2017) 'An economy for the 99%' *Oxfam Briefing Paper*. Available at www.oxfam.org

Parker, M. (1999) 'Capitalism, subjectivity and ethics: Debating labour process analysis' *Organization Studies* 20(1): 25–45.

Parker, M. (2002) *Against/Management*. Cambridge, Polity Press.

Parker, M. (2009) 'Angelic organisation: Hierarchy and the tyranny of heaven' *Organization Studies* 30(11): 1281–1299.

Parker, M. (2013) 'Beyond justification: Dietrologic and the sociology of critique' in P. Du Gay and G. Morgan (Eds.) *New Spirits of Capitalism? Crises, Justifications, and Dynamics*. Oxford, Oxford University Press, pp. 124–141.

Peppers, C. and Briskin, A. (2000) *Bringing Your Soul to Work: An Everyday Practice*. San Francisco, CA, Berrett Koehler.

Peters, T. and Waterman, R. (1982) *In Search of Excellence: Lessons from America's Best-Run Companies*. New York, Harper and Row.

Pew (2008) 'National Religious Landscape Survey Report.' Available at www.pewforum.org

Pew (2015) 'National Religious Landscape Survey Report.' Available at www.pewforum.org

Pfeffer, J. (1977) 'The ambiguity of leadership' *Academy of Management Review* January: 104–112.

Phillips, M. (1992) 'Corporate moral personhood and three conceptions of the corporation' *Business Ethics Quarterly* 2(4): 435–459.

Picketty, T. (2017) *Capital in the Twenty-First Century*. Harvard, Harvard University Press.

Pullen, A. and Rhodes, C. (Eds.) (2015) *The Routledge Companion to Ethics, Politics and Organizations*. London, Routledge.

Putnam, R. (2000) *Bowling Alone*. New York, Simon and Schuster.

Rhodes, C. and Wray-Bliss, E. (2013) 'The ethical difference of organization' *Organization* 20(1): 39–50.

Roberts, J. (2001) 'Corporate governance and the ethics of Narcissus' *Business Ethics Quarterly* 11(1): 109–127.

Roberts, J. (2003) 'The manufacture of corporate social responsibility: Constructing corporate sensibility' *Organization* 10: 249–266.

Roberts, J., Sanderson, P., Barker, R. and Hendry, J. (2006) 'In the mirror of the market: The disciplinary effects of company/fund manager meetings' *Accounting, Organizations and Society* 31(3): 277–294.

Roberts, M. (2017) 'Rick Perry said fossil fuels could help stop sexual assault. Oops' *Washington Post*, November 2.

Rose, N. (1989) *Governing the Soul: The Shaping of the Private Self*. London, Routledge.

Rose, N. (1991) 'Governing by numbers: Figuring out democracy' *Accounting, Organizations and Society* 16(7): 673–692.

Rose, N. (1999) *Governing the Soul*, Second Edition. London, Free Association Books.

Rothschild, E. (1994) 'Adam Smith and the invisible hand' *American Economic Review* 84(2): 319–322, in P. Oslington (Ed.) *The International Library of Critical Writings in Economics 167: Economics and Religion*, Volume 1. Edward Elgar, Cheltenham, pp. 288–291.

Roy, A. (2014) *Capitalism: A Ghost Story*. Chicago, Haymarket Books.

Sadler-Smith, E., Akstinaite, V., Robinson, G. and Wray, T. (2017) 'Hubristic leadership: A review' *Leadership* 13(5): 525–548.

Santoro, G., Wood, M., Merlo, L., Anastasi, G., Tomasello, F. and Germano, A. (2009) 'The anatomic location of the soul from the heart, through the brain, to the whole body, and beyond' *Neurosurgery* 65(4): 633–643.

Saul, J. (1997) *The Unconscious Civilisation*. Ringwood, Penguin.

Schwartz, M. (2000) 'Why ethical codes constitute an unconscionable regression' *Journal of Business Ethics* 23: 173–184.

Sennet, R. (1998) *The Corrosion of Character*. New York, W. W. Norton.

Sherwood, S. (2002) 'How to mix business and the Bible' *Chief Executive*, November 1, 183: 15.

Siedentop, L. (2014) *Inventing the Individual: The Origins of Western Liberalism*. London, Penguin Random House.

Singer, P. (2004) *The President of Good and Evil: The Convenient Ethics of George W. Bush*. New York, Dutton.

Skinner, D. (2013) 'Foucault, subjectivity and ethics: Towards a self-forming subject' *Organization* 20(6): 904–923.

Smith, A. (1759[2013]) *The Theory of Moral Sentiments*. Dallas, Economic Classics.

Smith, A. (1776) *An Inquiry into the Nature and Causes of the Wealth of Nations*, Book 1, Chapter 8, Paragraph 36. Available at https://en.wikisource.org/wiki/The_Wealth_of_Nations

Soares, C. (2003) 'Corporate versus individual moral responsibility' *Journal of Business Ethics* 46: 143–150.

Sørensen, B., Spolstra, S., Höpfl, H. and Critchley, S. (2012) 'Theology and organization' *Organization* 19(3): 267–279.

Spence, L. and Rinaldi, L. (2014) 'Governmentality in accounting and accountability: A case study of embedding sustainability in a supply chain' *Accounting, Organizations and Society* 39(6): 433–452.

Stephens, K. (2016) *Think Like Jesus: A Five Week Devotional for Lady Bosses*. Scotts Valley, Cal, CreateSpace Independent Publishing Platform.

Stewart, E. (2018) 'How does a company's CEO pay compare to its workers'? Now you can find out.' Available at https://www.vox.com/policy-and-politics/2018/4/8/17212796/ceo-pay-ratio-corporate-governance-wealth-inequality.

Stiegler, B. (2006[2014]) *The Lost Spirit of Capitalism*. Cambridge, Polity Press.

Sullivan, K. and Delaney, H. (2016) 'A femininity that "giveth and taketh away": The prosperity gospel and postfeminism in the neoliberal economy' *Human Relations* 70(7): 836–859.

Sutton, J. (2013) 'Soul and body in seventeenth-century British philosophy' in P. Anstey (Eds.) *The Oxford Handbook of British Philosophy in the Seventeenth Century*. Oxford, Oxford University Press.

Taylor, C. (2007) *A Secular Age*. Cambridge, MA, Harvard University Press.

Taylor, F. W. (1911) 'The Principles of Scientific Management'. Available at www.ibiblio.org

Thompson, P., Smith, C. and Ackroyd, S. (2000) 'If ethics is the answer, you are asking the wrong question' *Organization Studies* 21: 1149–1158.

Tracey, P., Phillips, N. and Lounsbury, M. (2014) 'Taking religion seriously in the study of organizations' in P. Tracey, N. Phillips and M. Lounsbury (Eds.) *Religion and Organization Theory: Research in the Sociology of Organizations*. Bingley, Emerald.

Union of Concern Scientists (2015) *The Climate Deception Dossiers: Internal Fossil Fuel Industry Memos Reveal Decades of Corporate Disinformation*. Available at www.ucusa.org

Walker, S. (2010) 'Child accounting and the "handling of human souls"' *Accounting, Organizations and Society* 35(6): 628–657.

Waterman, A. (2002) 'Economics as theology: Adam Smith's wealth of nations' *Southern Economic Journal* 68(4): 907–921 in P. Oslington (Ed.) *The International Library of Critical Writings in Economics 167: Economics and Religion*, Volume 1. Edward Elgar, Cheltenham, pp. 321–335.

Watson, T. (2003) 'Ethical choice in managerial work: The scope for moral choices in an ethically irrational world' *Human Relations* 56: 167–185.

Weber, M. (1930[2001]) *The Protestant Ethic and the Spirit of Capitalism*. London, Routledge.

Weiskopf, R. and Willmott, H. (2013) 'Ethics as critical practice: The "Pentagon Papers", deciding responsibly, truth-telling, and the unsettling of organizational morality' *Organization Studies* 34(4): 469–493.

Whyte, W. H. (1956) *The Organization Man*. New York, Simon and Schuster.

Willmott, H. (1993) 'Strength is ignorance, slavery is freedom: Managing culture in modern organizations' *Journal of Management Studies* 30(4): 515–552.

Willmott, H. (2013) 'When political economy becomes culturalized . . . ' in P. Du Gay and G. Morgan (Eds.) *New Spirits of Capitalism? Crises, Justifications, and Dynamics*. Oxford, Oxford University Press, pp. 98–123.

Wray-Bliss, E. (2002) 'Abstract ethics, embodied ethics: The strange marriage of Foucault and positivism in LPT' *Organization* 9(1): 5–39.

Wray-Bliss, E. (2009) 'Ethics: Critique, ambivalence and infinite responsibilities (unmet)' in M. Alvesson, T. Bridgman and H. Willmott (Eds.) *The Oxford Handbook of Critical Management Studies*. Oxford, Oxford University Press, pp. 267–285.

Wray-Bliss, E. (2012) 'Leadership and the deified/demonic: A cultural critique of CEO sanctification' *Business Ethics: A European Review* 21(4): 434–449.

Wray-Bliss, E. (2013) 'A crisis of leadership: Towards an anti-sovereign ethics of organisation' *Business Ethics: A European Review* 22(1): 86–101.

Wray-Bliss, E. (2016) 'Ethical philosophy, organization studies and good suspicions' in H. Willmott, et al. *The Routledge Companion to Philosophy in Organization Studies*. London, Routledge, pp. 51–65.

Zellner, W. (2001) 'Derring-do in the corner office' *Business Week*, February 12.

Zenoff, D. (2013) *The Soul of the Organization: How to Ignite Employee Engagement and Productivity at Every Level*. New York, Apress.

Zimbardo, P. (2008) *The Lucifer Effect*. New York, Random House.

# Index

Printed in the United States
by Baker & Taylor Publisher Services

Printed in the United States
by Baker & Taylor Publisher Services